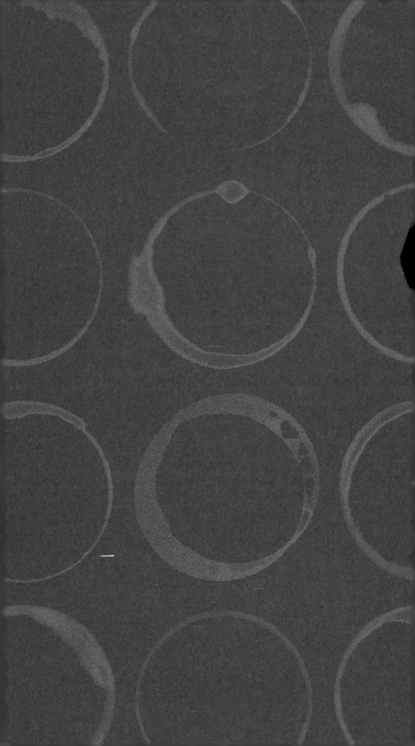

TOP 100 WINES UNDER $20

# Had a Glass
# 2016

## JAMES NEVISON

appetite
by RANDOM HOUSE

Appetite by Random House® and colophon are
registered trademarks of Penguin Random House LLC.

Library and Archives of Canada Cataloguing in Publication is available upon request

ISBN: 978-0-14-752973-2
eBook ISBN: 978-0-14-752974-9

Printed and bound in the USA

Published in Canada by Appetite by Random House®,
a division of Penguin Random House Canada Limited

www.penguinrandomhouse.ca

10 9 8 7 6 5 4 3 2 1

appetite
by RANDOM HOUSE

Penguin
Random
House

# CONTENTS

# A Brief Guide to Wine Enjoyment

## Ten Years of Wining!

The 2016 edition heralds the 10th anniversary of the Had a Glass series. This is a remarkable feat. After all, 99% of the wines for sale on shelves nowadays don't last 10 years. So it is both an exciting and humbling vintage for Had a Glass and shows read-ers' continued thirst for finding solid, everyday wine enjoyment.

Turning 10 offers good occasion for reflection. Along this wine journey, how many corks have been popped? How many screw caps have been twisted? How many glasses have been poured? A copious quantity, to be sure, but more importantly are the memories of good times shared over good meals with great people.

Though the actual count is forgotten, a look back across the *Had a Glass* years reveals some interesting numbers. In 2006, the inaugural edition featured 39 white wines, 48 reds, six aperitifs and fortifieds, a sad five bottles of sparkling, and an even sadder two options for rosé. By 2015, the bubbly and pink wines were better represented in the Top 100 (11 and five, respectively), with the whites checking in at 33 bottles and the reds at 44. Really, these numbers highlight how *Had a Glass* has always reflected the evolution in everyday wine enjoyment.

Over the past decade, wine consumption in Canada has risen drastically. We are drinking more—and better—wine (according to the latest figures, per capita wine consumption in Canada is expected to reach 16.4 litres by 2018[*]), and along with this increased thirst has come an increased hankering for wine knowledge. Wine consumers are more sophisticated and savvy than ever before, and in response the selection of wine in the marketplace continues to diversify. And this, ultimately, makes all the continued cork popping and screw-cap twisting worthwhile.

So cheers and thanks to all you thirsty readers who have made it possible to toast *Had a Glass* turning 10!

## For Best Results

*Had a Glass* wades through the muck and murky liquid to point out 100 wines worth sipping. Consider it a vinous compass to keep you from getting lost in the wine aisles. Better yet, all the wines featured on these pages sell for under $20. Because wine is meant for everyday enjoyment, and every meal deserves a glass of wine.

*Had a Glass* is filled with the straight wine goods. Each wine is here for a reason, whether it is perfect for patio sipping, pairs remarkably with salmon, or simply inspires engagement in impromptu conversation. The wines come from all over the

---

[*] VINEXPO, *World Wine and Spirits Market with an Outlook to 2018*

globe and represent a broad mix of grape varieties. There are reds and whites, not to mention rosés and sparkling, even a few fortified wines! It's true wine diversity, and true wine value.

Had a Glass is easy to use: pick a page, read the blurb, get the wine, and see what you think. Repeat.

But remember: wine is best enjoyed in moderation.
Know your limit and always have a safe way to get home.
Such is the path to true wine appreciation.

## Caveat Emptor and Carpe Diem!

Had a Glass goes out of the way to select wines that are widely available. Everyone deserves good wine, no matter what your postal code. While every effort is made to ensure prices and vintages are correct at publication, good wine buys sell out, and wines are subject to price variances and vintage changes.

It is recommended to use this book as a starting point for your wine adventures. Great bottles are out there, and as with all things worth searching for, the fun is in the hunt.

## Wine, Barcoded

In a nod to interactivity, Had a Glass features barcodes for each wine. Given the proliferation of smartphones there are all sorts of uses for this handy addition. Using the growing number of available wine "apps," you can scan the barcodes to locate stores and availability for each wine. Or scan your favourite bottles to create your own personalized wine-tasting journal!

## A Word about Value

"Value" is at best squishy and hard to pin down. Value is personal. And like scoring wine on a 100-point scale, it's tough for an objective framework to try to prop up subjective tastes. But whether you're after price rollbacks at a big-box store or hand-made designer goods, true value occurs when returns exceed expectations.

**How is value applied in Had a Glass?**
Most of the time the budget and bank account set a comfortable limit of my wine allotment at $20. On occasion I may spend more, but overall I toe the line. From research I know the majority of you feel the same. We all love great $18 bottles of wine. But we love cracking into a tasty $12 bottle even more!

Had a Glass celebrates wines that give you the best bottle for your buck: the $10 wine that seems like it should cost $15, the $15 bottle that stands out, and the $20 wine that knocks your socks off. Wine should be an everyday beverage, not a luxury—an enjoyable accessory to good living.

# How to Taste Wine

Drinking wine and tasting wine are two different pastimes. Now, there's nothing wrong with simply wanting to open a bottle, pour a glass, and carry on. Indeed, most of the time this is standard protocol. Company has arrived and dinner is on the table and away we go!

But if you're ready to take your relationship with wine to the next level, it's time to commit to proper tasting technique. This permits a complete sensory evaluation of the wine in your glass, and I promise that it will add to your wine enjoyment as well.

You've likely heard the motto that a good wine is "a wine you like." Sure, at the end of the day taste is subjective and personal opinion matters. But what really makes a wine good? After you understand how to taste wine, you'll be equipped to make that call.

# The Four Steps

There's no need to overcomplicate wine tasting. Nothing is more boring than listening to some wine blowhard drone on at length about the laundry list of aromas they detect, or slurp on for minutes as they attempt to pinpoint precise acidity and residual sugar levels. First impressions are often the best. Tasting wine is not a competition. It should be fun, which means yes, smile as you swirl and sip.

Here's the wine-tasting process in four simple steps:

### Step 1: The look

You can learn a lot simply by looking at a wine. Tilt the wineglass away from you and observe its colour, ideally against a white background (a blank sheet of paper works in a pinch). White wines appear pallid straw to deep gold, and reds typically range from light ruby to the dark crimson of a royal's ceremonial robe—even at times the neon purple of grape Gatorade. A wine's colour can also hint at its age. Young white wines often have the brilliant sheen of white gold, a shine that mellows as the years pass and the wine darkens overall. On the other hand, red wines lighten as they age, superimposing amber and auburn tones on sombre claret. Also consider that while most wines are nearly transparent in the glass, an unfiltered wine may appear slightly cloudy with sediment.

### Step 2: The swirl

To draw out a wine's aromas, give the glass a swirl. Use the base of a table for secure swirling, or raise your wineglass up high for an air swirl. Before you know it, you'll be swirling every glass in front of you, even if it holds water. The swirl not only helps release the aromas of a wine, it paints the sides of the glass with the wine's tears, or legs. These are the droplets that form around the wineglass and leisurely—or rapidly—make their way to the reservoir waiting at the bottom of the vessel. But note that while a wine's legs are fun to look at, they merely indicate texture and viscosity from residual sugars or alcohol, and don't necessarily suggest a wine's quality.

### Step 3: The smell
Don't be afraid to put your nose right into the glass—wine tasting is not chemistry class and we need not adhere to a waft test. Smelling is wine intimacy, and a deep inhale will reveal what the wine is about. Many wine tasters feel the smell is the most important step in "tasting" wine, with scent seemingly hardwired to our mind.

### What are you smelling?
It's not me, it's the Cabernet! Many factors contribute to a wine's aromas, or smells. A wine can have myriad aromas of fruit (citrus, berries, melons, mango), which may at first seem odd considering wine is made from just grapes. Wine can smell of place too, be it sun-baked earth, rain-slaked slate, or even horsey barnyard. Of course, the winemaker and winemaking process can also influence a wine's aromas, from the smoke, vanilla, and spice imbued from oak to the yeasty brioche goodness imparted from barrel fermentation and sur lie aging.

It's also important to remember that smell is quite personal. Your apricot may be my peach. And I find the more wines you taste, the more comfortable you become addressing aromas. Further, it's not a contest to come up with as many olfactory adjectives as possible—though creativity can be applied in determining what's that smell. (See box on page 10 for examples.)

### Step 4: The taste
Finally, take a generous sip of wine (it's fine to slurp as you sip, just as you would a mouthful of steaming ramen noodles!). Swirl it in your mouth. Swish it in your cheeks. Consider the wine's consistency and texture; this is what's referred to as a wine's body. Let your tongue taste the different elements of the wine: any sweetness from residual sugars, any tartness from acid, or any bitterness from alcohol. Tannins may dry your gums, making you pucker. Spitting is optional.

**Wine Aromas**

Commonly used words to describe wine aromas:

Unusual-sounding (but actually used) wine aromas:

| | |
|---|---|
| citrus | cat pee |
| berry | wet stone |
| peach | burnt match |
| melon | rubber band |
| mango | cut grass |
| bell pepper | barnyard |
| flowers | baking bread |
| olive | diesel |
| nut | Tupperware |
| caramel | sweat |
| vanilla | cheese |
| oak | bacon |
| smoke | cracked black pepper |
| earth | tobacco |
| fig | tar |

## Understanding Body and Finish

Just like hair, wine has body. I find it easiest to think of a wine's body as its texture. And I still find the best analogy for understanding "body" is to think about milk. The consistency may be thin like skim milk (light-bodied) or it may be thick like cream (full-bodied). In the middle of the spectrum we have medium-bodied, the 2% milk of the wine world. Light-, medium-, and full-bodied are the three basic descriptions used, and it's perfectly acceptable to employ a range when describing a wine, say light- to medium-bodied for example.

However, all good things must come to an end, and a wine's finish refers to the lingering flavours and taste sensations that remain after it's been spit (or swallowed). The jargon is surprisingly simple to describe a wine's finish, which is generally described as short, medium, or long. That said, there's no simple formula for delineating each category. No point in getting out the stopwatch and clocking a wine's finish. In fact, there's no point in getting overly hung up on a wine's finish; better to move on to the next sip.

## Wine-Tasting Tips

• Take notes! Whether you carry a leather-bound wine journal, scribble on a paper napkin, or tap away on a smartphone, take wine notes whenever you can. At the very least, jot down the winery name, grape variety, the year, and a thumbs-up or thumbs-down beside it. (No, you will not remember the wine the next day, other than perhaps that the bottle had a bird on the label.)

• When it comes to glasses, go big. And don't pour it more than half full. This will allow for proper swirling (as per Step 2).

• Practice makes perfect. Like you needed more motivation.

• But it's best not to practise alone. Tasting wine with a companion or group is a great way to gain multiple opinions and perspectives.

## Suggested Wine Flights for Wine-Tasting Practice

Wine flights are a great way to practise tasting wine. The more wines you try, the better your frame of reference and the larger your internal wine database. A "flight" of wine lines up small pours of a few wines that share a common theme, allowing for great side-by-side comparison. It's like taking three pairs of jeans into the changing room!

Here are three wine flights for wine-tasting practice:

## Flight 1: Try the Pinot trio

Which Pinot are you: black, grey, or white? Pinot is a family of grapes; in fact, Pinot Gris and Pinot Blanc (as well as Pinot Meunier) are only a few examples of the many mutations of their parent grape, Pinot Noir. Can you detect the lineage as you taste through this trio of Pinots?

• Hester Creek Pinot Blanc, British Columbia (page 71)
• Pfaffenheim Pfaff Pinot Gris, France (page 81)
• Viña Tabalí Reserva Pinot Noir, Chile (page 126)

## Flight 2: Sip savvy Sauvignon Blanc

Sauvignon Blanc has become a versatile, well-loved white wine. It's as at home atop the dining table as it is out on the patio. And while most Sauvignon Blancs are made to be enjoyed young while they're bursting with fresh fruit and acidity, it doesn't mean you can't take a contemplative tasting moment to enjoy the flavourful nuances of the grape in this Sauv Blanc flight:

• Babich Sauvignon Blanc, New Zealand (page 80)
• Casas del Bosque Sauvignon Blanc, Chile (page 70)
• Robert Mondavi Winery Fumé Blanc, United States (page 85)

## Flight 3: Get fortified!

For many, fortified wines are not the first potable option that springs to mind. Yet they are surprisingly versatile and varied, offering a unique experience that can really add to wine enjoyment—whether served before, during, or after a meal. Cut through the fortified wine mystery with this diverse and delicious trifecta:

• Lustau Puerto Fino Sherry, Spain (page 158)
• Florio Vecchioflorio Marsala Superiore Dolce, Italy (page 159)
• Warre's Warrior Reserve Port (page 154)

## It's the Wine's Fault

Unfortunately, there is likely a point in your wine-tasting career when you'll encounter a faulty wine. That said, with today's high-quality standards, in general there's less bad wine out there. Given our differing thresholds of perception, wine faults may be more or less apparent. But if you open a bottle and think something's funky, it might be due to one of these common wine faults:

- **"Corked" wine or cork taint.** Technically caused by a naturally occurring compound called 2,4,6-trichloroanisole (TCA) found in the oak bark used to produce corks, and attributed to improper cork sanitation. At worst, cork taint can leave a wine smelling and tasting mouldy like wet newspaper, but it can also mute flavours and aromas in general.
- **Oxidation.** Too much exposure to oxygen! A wine is particularly susceptible to oxidation after fermentation has completed and carbon dioxide levels have waned. Oxidized wine usually appears brownish in colour and smells stale.
- **Volatile acidity.** When fermentation goes awry, volatile acidity (VA) is usually the end result. VA shows itself in two main ways, through ethyl acetate, which smells like nail polish remover, or acetic acid— good ol' vinegar!
- **Too much $SO_2$.** The overwhelming majority of wines contain sulphur dioxide, which serves as a preservative and keeps wine stable. Some sulphur dioxide occurs naturally during the winemaking process, but most wineries also add sulphur dioxide. How much is a question of principle and philosophy, but if your wine smells like rotten eggs, it's faulty. If it has just a hint of sulphur dioxide, like a just-lit match, it may blow off and be fine.
- **Brettanomyces.** A funky, naturally occurring yeast behind such colourful wine descriptions as "Band-Aid" and "sweaty horse." Brettanomyces, or Brett, comes from the vineyard and can establish itself in the winery and winery equipment, especially if proper sanitation is not employed. But here's the rub: Brett gets personal. Some wine tasters like a little Brettanomyces in their wine and feel it adds character and complexity—but too much is funky gone off the railroad tracks.

# How to Buy Wine

Buying a bottle of wine shouldn't raise heart rates or cause palms to sweat. Wine is fun, and strolling through your local bottle shop should be a joy. Wine-buying confidence has come a long way in the past decade, but there's no harm in offering a few tips to help your troll of the wine aisles.

## Navigating the Wine Store

The typical liquor store or wine shop organizes its wine by country. This is helpful categorization if you're feeling geographic, but somewhat awkward if you want a Chardonnay and have to run around comparing one country's offering with another. Things can get particularly unruly if you head to a section with

French or Italian wines and are confronted with regional names emblazoned across the labels instead of the types of grape. No reason to panic (in fact, many traditional wine labels are starting to include the grapes along with the region). Get to know where certain grapes come from, and you'll be sleuthing through bottles in no time.

### Where does wine come from?

Grapes are grown and wine is made in well over 100 countries. Entire books are written to cover the various wine regions of the world. This will not be another one. However, a quick primer can provide down-and-dirty generalizations to help you on your way to grape globetrotting.

### Old World vs. New World

Before even delving into specific countries, it's important to discuss the Old World and New World of wine. Broadly speaking, the Old World refers to those countries around the Mediterranean basin that have thousands of years of grape-growing and wine-drinking history. We're talking France, Italy, Spain, Portugal, Germany, Austria, Hungary, Greece, et al. The rest of the globe's viticultural hotspots fall into the New World camp.

Traditionally, Old World wines have been typified as more austere and terroir, or place, driven. This is why the wines are usually labelled according to region rather than grape. New World wines tend to get labelled fruit-forward, ripe, and extroverted.

Of course, generalizations are handy but simplistic, and today the line between Old and New World has certainly blurred. You'll find French wines with cute marketing and grape names prominently displayed, and you'll find Chilean bottles touting adherence to Old World–style dry farming and wild yeast fermentation.

The key take-away? It's great to be a wine drinker in this Postmodern World, as the quality (and type) of wine widely available has never been better.

# GrapeWHERE

So what happened to the Pinot Gris and Merlot on the label?
Don't fret if you don't see familiar grape names listed on the front of that
bottle from _____ {insert "Old World" country}.
Just remember this is where you'll find different grapes:

WHERE                          Grape(s)

**White wines**
Bordeaux, France               Sémillon and Sauvignon Blanc
Burgundy, France               Chardonnay
Cava, Spain                    Macabeo, Parellada, and Xarel-lo
Champagne, France              Chardonnay, Pinot Noir, and Pinot
                               Meunier
Côtes du Rhône, France         Roussanne, Marsanne, and Viognier
Gavi, Italy                    Cortese
Mosel, Germany                 Riesling
Rioja, Spain                   Viura (a.k.a. Macabeo)

**Red wines**
Barbaresco, Italy              Nebbiolo
Barolo, Italy                  Nebbiolo
Beaujolais, France             Gamay
Bordeaux, France               Cabernet Sauvignon, Merlot, and
                               Cabernet Franc (and maybe a little
                               Malbec and Petit Verdot)
Burgundy, France               Pinot Noir
Cahors, France                 Malbec
Chianti, Italy                 Sangiovese
Côtes du Rhône, France         Mostly Syrah and Grenache, with
                               Carignan, Mourvèdre, and Cinsault
Rioja, Spain                   Tempranillo, Garnacha
Valpolicella, Italy            Corvina

## Understanding Wine Labels

What's written on the wine label counts. You can learn a lot about a wine before you buy. The trick is to know what's worth reading. Wine label literacy can go a long way toward increasing wine enjoyment.

### Wine or winery name

Back in the day, the name would be a château or domaine, or possibly it would be a proprietary name that was used by a wine-making co-operative. While these labels are still out there, brand names, animal species, and focus-grouped marketing buzzwords are now gracing wine bottles—all in an effort to help you remember what you drank.

### Vintage

The year printed on the label is the year the grapes were grown. There are good years and bad years, typically determined by weather conditions.

The vintage is included for the wines reviewed in *Had a Glass*. Where no vintage is listed, the wine is "non-vintage," meaning it's been made from a mix of years. Non-vintage is quite common for sparkling and fortified wines.

### Alcohol

Generally expressed as "alcohol by volume" (ABV), this tells you how much wine you can taste before the line between "tasting" and "drinking" becomes blurred. Or blurry. As a rough guide, higher alcohol content (14% is high, anything above 14.5% is really high) suggests a heftier, more intense wine. On the other side of the ABV spectrum, wines with less than 11% will often be off-dry (slightly sweet). High alcohol doesn't connote a better wine. It's all about balance, and regardless of the number, a wine shouldn't have the grating bitterness of alcohol—it's not supposed to taste like a whisky shot.

### Grape variety

You pick up a can of soup and it's "mushroom" or "tomato." On a wine bottle you often see the grape variety: Malbec or Merlot or Chardonnay, to mention a few. These are your single varietal wines, as opposed to "blended" wines, which combine two or more grapes (such as Cabernet-Merlot and Sémillon–Sauvignon Blanc). Keep in mind that single varietal wines are no better than blends, and vice versa. Preference is dictated by your taste buds.

### Appellation

Or, where the grapes came from. Old World wine often gives you the appellation instead of the grape variety. But appellations will also inform you about the grapes in the bottle. (See the chart on page 20.) Take an example from Spain. "Rioja," arguably the country's most famous appellation, describes where the grapes originated, and because Spanish appellation laws state only certain grapes are authorized in certain areas, the name also hints at what grapes made the wine. So, appellations (Burgundy, Chianti, Mosel) also help to define taste.

**Appellations Around the World**

When it comes to appellations, each country has its own terminology. Here are the common formal designations you'll see on wine labels, which indicate that the grapes used to produce the wine are from the demarcated region.

| Country | Regional Designation |
|---|---|
| France | Appellation d'Origine Contrôlée (AOC or AC) |
| France | Vin de pays (VDP) |
| Germany | Qualitätswein mit Prädikatswein (QmP) |
| Germany | Qualitätswein bestimmter Anbaugebiete (QbA) |
| Italy | Denominazione di Origine Controllata (DOC) |
| Italy | Denominazione di Origine Controllata e Garantita (DOCG) |
| Italy | Indicazione geografica tipica (IGT) |
| Spain | Denominación de Origen (DO) |
| Spain | Denominación de Origen Calificada (DOCa) |
| Portugal | Denominação de Origem Controlada (DOC) |
| Chile | Denominación de Origen (DO) |
| Australia | Geographical Indication (GI) |
| South Africa | Wine of Origin (WO) |
| United States | American Viticultural Area (AVA) |
| Canada | Designated Viticultural Area (DVA), regulated by the Vintners Quality Alliance (VQA) |

## Occasional Wine

Of course, regardless of how the wines are organized, we often buy a bottle for a certain occasion, be it to pair with Mom's meat loaf or to celebrate Sarah's birthday. This is a logical way to buy wine, especially—ahem—for the occasional wine drinker. But do you match the wine to the food or match the food to the wine? The answer will affect your wine-buying decision.

# GrapeWHEN

| Grape | WHEN |
|---|---|
| **White wines** | |
| Chardonnay | roast chicken, crab drizzled in butter |
| Chenin Blanc | pasta alfredo, satay |
| Gewürztraminer | curry, salad |
| Pinot Blanc | shrimp cocktail, minestrone |
| Pinot Gris | smoked salmon, brie |
| Riesling | rillette, turkey |
| Sauvignon Blanc | goat cheese, fried chicken |
| Sémillon | clams, pasta primavera |
| Torrontés | on its own, Peking duck |
| Viognier | halibut, ginger beef |
| Champagne | anytime! |
| | |
| **Red wines** | |
| Cabernet Franc | pork roast, vegetarian lasagna |
| Cabernet Sauvignon | porterhouse, kebabs |
| Carmenère | eggplant, grilled beef |
| Gamay | tacos, turkey |
| Malbec | venison, mixed grill |
| Merlot | Camembert, mushrooms |
| Pinotage | bison, goulash |
| Pinot Noir | salmon, duck |
| Sangiovese | lasagna, pizza |
| Shiraz | lamb, pecorino |
| Tempranillo | steak, bacon |
| Zinfandel | burgers, teriyaki |
| Port | in a cozy chair with a book |

## Feel the Wine

There's nothing wrong with getting emotional with wine, and another buying strategy is to match the wine to a mood. When staring at a wall of wine wondering what to put in the basket, consult your mood ring or do a quick self-emotive audit. Perhaps a bold evening calls for an aggressive wine, just as a mellow affair may require an equally subdued bottle? Looking for a little comfort? Head back to the tried-and-true.

| Feeling | Try | From |
|---|---|---|
| adventurous | Riesling | Germany, B.C., or Australia |
| mellow | Pinot Noir | France or Oregon |
| assertive | Shiraz | Australia or Washington |
| apathetic | Chardonnay | anywhere |
| it's complicated | Cabernet blend | Chile or Argentina |

## Broadening Wine Horizons

While still on the topic of feelings, if you're feeling a bit adventurous, now is the perfect time to experiment with a never-before-tasted wine.

| Like | Try | From |
|---|---|---|
| Malbec | Pinotage | South Africa |
| Cabernet Sauvignon | Tempranillo | Spain |
| Shiraz | Nero d'Avola | Italy |
| Chardonnay | Viognier | France |
| Sauvignon Blanc | Grüner Veltliner | Austria |
| Gewürztraminer | Ehrenfelser | B.C. |

## The Role of Vintages

Just when you think you're getting to know the nuances of a particular wine, along comes a new vintage! This is in fact one of the more exciting aspects of fermented grape juice. Wine is an agricultural product, subject to the annual vagaries of

Mother Nature. If you want your wine to be the same year in and year out, you may as well buy Welch's. But how important is a wine's vintage?

A general rule is that it's easier to make good wine in a great year, but great grape-growers and winemakers can make good wine every year. A good vintage typically means great to ideal growing conditions: no untimely frosts, plenty of sun to encourage full and even ripening, and so on. That said, in a poor vintage, steps can be taken to minimize negative impacts.

So the vintage of a wine matters, but not to the point that it should limit your wine purchase. Indeed, for everyday wine drinking, vintages are usually not really considered. Now if you were investing in wine or looking to purchase bottles at an auction it would be a different story, but those aren't the types of wine you'll find in the pages of Had a Glass.

## Corks vs. Screw Caps

There was a time, and we're still talking the 21st century, when a significant proportion of wine drinkers would rather drink water than be seen sipping from a bottle of screw-capped wine. Thankfully it hasn't taken long for most to realize that pulling a cork out of a bottle is only romantic until the first corked bottle, which seems to happen when there is no backup bottle at hand! And with an estimated 5% of wines with a cork subject to taint, this is a failure rate no other industry would rightfully tolerate.

So unless you're looking to cellar a wine for a particularly lengthy period of time, or you're risk-seeking and own an impressive collection of corkscrews, embrace the screw cap as an effective, efficient flavour saver. Anyways, it's not like corks are going to completely disappear anytime soon. Just don't be afraid to buy a wine based on its topper!

## Returning Wine

If a wine is faulty, take it back! Generally this will be due to cork taint, though there is potential for other faults. (See page 13 for a review of common wine faults.) Just don't drink most of the bottle before bringing it back to the store! And no, it is not acceptable to return a wine simply because you do not like the way it tastes. Chalk it up to experience, take notes ruminating on your unmet expectations, and move on to the next bottle.

## Avoid a Wine Rut

Becoming a little too comfortable with a certain bottle? It's great to have favourite go-to wines, but remember that it's a wide wine world. If your wining has been monotonous of late, consider these strategies on your next trip to the wine store.

### Explore new wine frontiers

When you find yourself infatuated by a particular grape—be it cheerful Chenin Blanc or sumptuous Syrah—expand on your interest by seeking similar bottles from around the wine world.

Riesling is remarkably diverse, and thanks to its growing popularity it is increasingly being both enjoyed and produced around the world. For a quick global tour in your wineglass, start in Riesling's fabled home and heartland with Selbach (page 74), which hails from the steep-sloped Mosel region of Germany. Halfway around the world, and a 180-degree tur n in style, is the starkly dry Riesling from Wakefield (page 82), made with grapes grown in South Australia's Clare Valley. Finally, head back home for a completely different, decidedly sweet yet fresh and poised Late Harvest Riesling from South Okanagan's Gehringer Brothers (page 155).

### Get a lay of the land

Certain parts of the world make certain types of wine. Cooler-climate areas typically produce wines with higher levels of acidity, and conversely, warmer regions tend to produce riper grapes that manifest in rich, fruit-forward wines. This sense of place imbued in wine is one of the beverage's more enduring traits. Flipping through these pages, you'll see some great wine regions featured this year.

France, for example, is home to a disproportionate share of the world's renowned wine regions. From Burgundy to Bordeaux, not to mention Champagne and a myriad of subregions in the Rhône Valley, France's vineyards and wines have long captivated wine lovers (and wine collectors). While many bottles from these star areas are beyond the pages of *Had a Glass*, you can still get to know the diversity of France's appellations by sipping through the country. Start out west in the Loire with Marquis de la Tour's Brut (page 145). Next, head south to Mediterranean France with the lush Moillard Hugues le Juste Viognier (page 62) before ambling east to the Rhône Valley by way of Famille Perrin's peppery L'Andéol Rasteau (page 138).

### Trade up
A winery commonly makes different tiers of wines, akin to a vinous version of Toyota versus Lexus. *Had a Glass* is all about the everyday sipper, but if you like what you're test-driving, look for the luxury version. This year's edition features the delectable Langhe red from Beni di Batasiolo (page 123), which is ready to take on meals Monday through Friday without breaking the bank. But if you're looking for something a little more decadent and don't mind laying out more cash, this well-regarded northern Italian winery has the goods for you! Batasiolo only farms in Italy's Langhe region, which means they specialize in Nebbiolo, as highlighted in their bottles of Barbaresco (~$26), basic Barolo (~$35), or even the single-vineyard Boscareto Barolo (~$55).

# Alt Wine: Thinking Outside the Bottle

Now that the screw-cap debate has wound down, it's time to tackle a new frontier in wine packaging. Why are we so married to the wine bottle, anyways? After all, wine is made and mostly matured in either stainless steel tanks or oak barrels. Not to mention a heavy glass bottle is hardly the most efficient (nor environmental) means for storing wine in this day and age. Really, unless the motivation is about collecting wine and adding bottles to the cellar, there's no reason for bottle envy. Don't be surprised to see more alternative packages, from cask wines to wine on tap, arriving on shelves in the years to come.

## Cask wine

Cask wine is nothing new, though it is certainly likely to be an increasing trend. Also known as bag-in-box wine—the more descriptive albeit less romantic name—these nearly indestructible vessels not only make great backcountry travel partners, they're also more environmentally friendly and create an airtight seal to help keep wine fresh longer once it is opened. Incorporating a plastic bag encased in a cardboard box, cask wine typically comes in three- or four-litre formats—though smaller 1.5-litre casks are starting to appear. Unfortunately, particularly in North America, cask wine carries the stigma of being high-bulk, low-quality produce, but around the world casks are used to contain some serious juice (and in reality, often cask wine is the same wine that goes into a producer's glass bottles). The fact remains, cask wine is a great package for enjoying wine.

**Check out**
**Bota Box**
**2012 Old Vine Zinfandel**
**$34.79 for 3L**

Yes, it's four regular-sized bottles of wine stuffed into an easy-to-lug-around box! With a claim of keeping wine fresh for six weeks after opening, there's no doubt that this cask wine offers both economies of scale and unparalleled convenience. It will certainly make a statement plonked on the dinner table, though you may want to keep the box in the kitchen and pour into a decanter for classy table-side service. Waiting inside the box is a smooth Old Vines Zinfandel that certainly aims to please by offering the classic Zinfandel characteristics of sweet fruit and baking spice in a straightforward, round style. Pair with a pot of chili or campfire-grilled smokies in the backcountry.

Turkey chili

Grilled smokies

Patio/Picnic, Rock Out

 United States

# Aseptic Packaging, a.k.a. Tetra Paks

The issue with casks, of course, is that they still tend to be large volume packages. This is fine if the wine is intended for a restaurant or (very) large gathering, but three or four litres is a lot of wine, and even if the wine keeps for a longer period it's nice to have some variety (and food pairing versatility). Enter the Tetra Pak. This aseptic package pares things down to a manageable one-litre size while maintaining portability and a light weight. Heck, if it's good enough for all the fruit juice out there, it's good enough for everyday wine. Tetra Pak–packed wine has been available around the world for quite some time, although it's been slower coming to Canada. However, there are a few on offer on local shelves for sipping convenience.

**Check out**
**French Rabbit**
**Cabernet Sauvignon**
**$13.29 for 1L**

It's unbreakable, extremely quaffable, and when the Pak is empty, filled up with water, and then frozen, it makes a great ice block for the cooler. While French Rabbit is not the most complicated red available, it goes grape-to-grape with the majority of value-priced Cabernet out there, and the 1-litre Tetra Pak gives you an extra glass (or two) for the price. Ruby in colour, with ripe dark fruit, spice, and toasty oak, this medium-bodied gulper certainly goes down easy at the campsite, or on the boat, or anywhere else where packing glass is an issue.

 Donair

Raclette

 BYO, Winter Warmer

 France

## Wine on Tap

Wine on tap, essentially wine served on draught via stainless steel kegs, is being billed as the newest wine trend, but really it's only new to this part of the world. Throughout Europe, wine drinkers have long been able to pony up to the local wine depot or corner grocer with empty demijohn or Fanta bottle in tow for a quick fill. Granted, the kegs in question are usually huge plastic vats or oak barrels, and the wine on tap is typically everyday-drinking table wine.

The current push for wine on tap promotes both quality and locality, an approach that complements perspectives of sustainability quite nicely, particularly in western Canada. In British Columbia, given the proximity of Okanagan vineyards, it makes sense for many wineries to forego the bottling process in order to get wine to market as quick and conveniently as possible. So don't be surprised to soon see local Pinot Gris on tap next to the Pilsner and IPA!

### Check out

While regulations don't (yet) allow consumers to head down to the liquor store with refillable wine bottle in hand, wine on tap is becoming readily available at a growing number of restaurants. And a visit to the Vancouver Urban Winery located in the city's downtown east side really showcases draught wine. Not only is the facility responsible for getting an increasing number of winery's wares out of cask and into keg, the "urban winery" features a tasting bar equipped with 36 wines on tap!

# How to Enjoy Wine

Wine is like golf. There is a huge array of specialized accessories. But all you really need to play the game is a set of clubs and some balls. Likewise, all you really need to enjoy wine is a bottle and a glass. From there, it's up to you to decide how much you want to invest and how much shelf space you want to devote to storing wine paraphernalia.

## Glasses and Stemware

Crystal? Stemless? Plastic tumbler? Mason jar? The wineglass options are varied, and while not all glasses are created equal, drinking wine from any glass can be equally enjoyable.

It's true that you can buy a different glass tailor-made to each type of wine. While there is no harm in gathering a glass collection, it's definitely not a necessary pursuit to maximize your wine enjoyment. A set of good white and red glasses (Chardonnay- and Bordeaux-shaped make sense) will suffice, and a standardized ISO tasting glass is helpful to really take wine tasting seriously. But at the end of the day, when a wonderful meal is waiting on the table, a simple juice glass works as well!

### Good stemware has its benefits

- Swirling wine in the larger bowl common to fancy glasses does wonders for releasing a wine's aromas. And it's best to pour a few fingers at a time to get a proper swirl going.

- Holding a glass by its stem helps keep white wines chilled, and it also keeps grubby fingerprints off the glass!

- A glass with a thin rim certainly provides an elegant tactile sensation.

- The stemless wineglasses that have recently become popular may get marked up with fingerprints, but they fit great in the dishwasher!

## Decanters

After glasses, the next most important wine accessory is the decanter. It provides both form and function, and is a secret to getting the most out of your wine.

Decanters have typically been associated with old wines, and it is true that decanting old wines to remove the liquid from the sediment will keep your teeth clean. But how often do you find yourself drinking aged wine?

In these contemporary times, the best use of a decanter is as a wine time-machine! Use your decanter to decant young wines, allowing them to breathe. Most wines we buy are consumed young—often too young—and decanting will open these wines up, smoothing their fruit and revealing their true character. There's no magic formula for how long to decant a bottle before drinking, and don't be afraid to give the wine a vigorous shake, but as a general rule most red wines appreciate an hour in the decanter. Try "airing" lighter reds for half an hour. White wines don't really need to decant unless you just like the look of it

Anything can be used as a decanter, from a clean teapot to a juice jug. To get serious about your decanter, find a glass or crystal container with a wide base and a narrow opening. This facilitates swirling, makes for easier pouring, and looks styling on the table!

## Corkscrews

Butterfly

T-Bar

Waiter's Friend

Wars have been fought over broken corks. Well, perhaps not, but it certainly is disappointing when a cork is mangled and broken into bits at the hand(s) of a bad corkscrew. (Actually, wine—and the supply thereof—has certainly been a fixture in many wars over the years.)

A corkscrew does not have to be intricate or expensive: a good corkscrew simply needs a well-wound worm (the screw part that winds into the cork) and some decent mechanism for leverage. Avoid corkscrews with worms that resemble a drill bit or wood screw, as these culprits typically do more cork ripping than pulling. Past experience shows these latter worms are most often found on the so-called butterfly corkscrew.

Purists might opt for the good old-fashioned T-bar corkscrew, which certainly hints at nostalgia and can make quite the design statement when the worm is grafted to an old hunk of grapevine à la rustic French fashion. Just be ready for a firm forearm work-out, and be prepared to shove the wine bottle between your legs (or feet) for stability and leverage. Gadgetphiles may be drawn to the fancy, pneumatically assisted, and gear-operated corkscrews available, which work just fine but tend to cost the equivalent of a couple good bottles.

For the best all-around corkscrew there's none better than the waiter's friend. Resembling a pocket knife, this simple cork-screw is the go-to option for servers and sommeliers the world over. It tirelessly opens wine bottles, and usually includes a small knife for cutting through bottle foils as well as an inte-grated crown cap opener. The waiter's friend is cheap (they're pretty easy to find at thrift stores for a couple bucks) and effec-tive (never yet met a cork it couldn't beat), and makes you look like you mean wine business when looped around your belt.

## Collecting Wine

Starting a wine collection is a fantastic way to expand your wine enjoyment. Sure, a fancy cellar with custom millwork, temperature control, and cobwebs-placed-just-so is a beauti-ful thing, but the 99% of us that don't have the space, the resources, or the patience for such a cellar needn't be deterred from collecting wine.

Start your wine collection simply with a bottle each of red, white, and sparkling wine. Keep the white and bubbly in the fridge and replenish as required. This vinous triumvirate ensures you're prepared for any impromptu occasion. Add to this base collection by picking up bottles while travelling, or perhaps track down a wine you had at a restaurant and really enjoyed. The key is to tie the wines to personal experience, which will add to enjoyment when you finally get around to opening a bottle. If the wine will be consumed in a year or two, simply keep it displayed in your wine rack or in the corner of a closet.

Of course it's important to keep wine storage in perspective. More than 90% of wine sold today is made for drinking now (or in a week, three weeks, six months). There is wine for aging and there is wine for drinking, and this book is about the latter. But there's no denying that wine evolves as it gets older, and a wine that is made to cellar can metamorphose into a completely different beverage, replete with aroma and flavour nuances not permitted in young wine. Just make sure to do some research if you plan on buying wine to enjoy in decades to come.

### A Starter Cellar

Curious about aging wine? Just as raw denim takes time to meld and mould and come into its own, the maturing process can add real character to the right wine. Here is a mixed half-case culled from wines reviewed in this book. Put them in a box, place on its side, and shove away in the basement or seldom-used closet and see how they develop in three to five years.

1) Wakefield Riesling, Australia (page 82)
2) De Morgenzon DMZ Chardonnay, South Africa (page 83)
3) M. Chapoutier Les Vignes de Bila-Haut, France (page 121)
4) Pedra Cancela Dão Seleção de Eñologo, Portugal (page 134)
5) Beni di Batasiolo Langhe, Italy (page 123)
6) Tinhorn Creek Merlot, British Columbia (page 127)

## Wine-Serving Temperatures

| red wine | 18°C (65°F) | a bit below room temperature |
|---|---|---|
| white (and rosé wine) | 10°C (50°F) | 20 minutes out of the fridge |
| sparkling and sweet wine | 5°C (40°F) | straight from the fridge |

**Tips**

- The chart on the previous page provides general guidelines, but personal preference trumps suggestions.

- Lighter red wines (such as Gamay Noir and Valpolicella) are often enjoyable served a bit cooler, especially when the weather is warm. Conversely, richer white wines (such as Chardonnay) show more complexity served a little warmer than usual.

- Err on the side of serving a wine too cold. The bottle will always warm up as it sits on the table.

- If a wine is sweet, serving it cold will make it seem drier and more refreshing.

- All dessert wine should be served at fridge temperature, unless it's red—like port—in which case you should serve it at the same temperature as red wine.

## The Dregs, or Leftover Wine

It's true that wine starts to deteriorate once the bottle is opened and the wine is exposed to oxygen. But how much time do you have before the bottle goes bad? Generally, polishing off a bottle the following day—or if you must, even the day after—is fine.

Yes, there are strategies to postponing a wine's demise. All manner of vacuum pumps and inert-gas sprays are available to attempt keeping $O_2$ at bay. If you're wary of accumulating any more wine gadgets, you can simply replace the cork or cap and place the bottle in the fridge—whether white, pink, or red—to slow down the oxidation.

If all this sounds like a lot of effort, you may simply be better off breaking out a chunk of cheese and pouring the dregs around!

# Food and Wine

Wine without food is like treble without bass. Sure they can exist separately, but the two really work together to create a whole. Of course, put notes together willy-nilly and there's no guarantee of musicality. Same with wine. The food and pairing strategies below serve to help you find harmony in order to turn up the gastronomical stereo!

### Red meat
Serve red wine. "Red wine with red meat" is one adage that rings true. Beef, lamb, and game are hearty. They're full-flavoured and heavy. They're packed with protein. Red wines—especially Cabernet Sauvignon, Malbec, Merlot, and Syrah—follow the same traits. Plus, hearty red wines tend to contain more tannins

than other wines, and protein works wonders in smoothing out tannic wine.

## Poultry

*Serve fruity medium-bodied white wine.* Everyone likes chicken, right? And nothing beats a holiday-festooned turkey. Similarly, most people are happy with dry medium-bodied white wine. We're talking Pinot Gris, Sémillon, and friends. If you want to get creative, try sparkling wine.

## Pork

*Serve medium to rich whites, light to medium reds.* The "other" white meat can take to a lot of different wines. An off-dry Riesling goes gangbusters with roast pork (don't forget the applesauce), or if your wine choice swings red, opt for a lighter rosso from Italy's Veneto region, or Gamay Noir in general. Ground pork stir-fried with an Asian twist is a prime partner for exotic, aromatic Torrontés. The bottom line is that pork is highly wine-friendly; it really depends on how you sauce the swine.

## Fish

*With delicate fish serve light to medium white wine.* The way you cook the fish makes all the difference. The delicacy of a poached fish needs a delicate wine like Pinot Blanc or Soave. If you're baking, seek a bit more texture from a white Bordeaux blend or Pinot Grigio. Frying in a glorious sea of butter? Open a Chardonnay or a sparkling wine. Overall a good strategy to follow is: the oilier the fish, the heavier the wine can be.

*With firm fish serve medium white or light to medium red wine.* Any fish that can be sold in "steaks" qualifies in this camp. For example, wild B.C. salmon has plenty of flavour, and it takes a wine with extra heft to get along with it. Likewise, halibut is no shrimp. White-wise, try both oaked or unoaked Chardonnays and Viognier. Red-wise, try a Pinot Noir. And don't forget rosé.

### Shellfish

Serve *light white wine.* Look to fresh, crisp wines—just how you want your shellfish to be! Consider how lemon or lime are often employed with seafood to perk things up, then consider wines with comparably high acidity. It's also safe to bet on white wines with no, or neutral, oak flavour. Albariño, Chenin Blanc, and Riesling are bivalve- and crustacean-friendly. Sparkling wine is another refreshing, go-to option.

### Vegetarian

Serve *wine similar in flavour and texture to the veg.* No offence to soy protein, but what's up with tofurkey and meatless meat substitutes? Vegetarianism and veganism are noble pursuits in their own right and can be celebrated as such (with wine). Vegetables, grains, legumes—all pair with vino. Simply consider flavours and texture. Earthy, hearty dishes featuring mushroom or eggplant go great with heartier, earthy reds. Lemon-splashed quinoa salad fares well with citrusy Sauvignon Blanc.

### Spicy

Serve *fruity, off-dry, and lower-alcohol white wine.* Wine and spice can make strange bedfellows. Keep the capsaicin in relative check, and a slightly sweet, fruity wine like Gewürztraminer or an aromatic white blend will show through the spice. But if the food is heavy on jalapeño, go with beer.

### Dessert

Serve *red or white wine that's sweeter than the dessert.* If the wine is too dry, the sweet dessert will make it seem even drier. And blander. Look for fortified wines like port and Marsala that are sweet but not cloying, or a lively and spritzy Moscato d'Asti to keep things light.

Oh, and a word about chocolate: it's harder to pair the cacao than you think. Stick to quality dark chocolate and still heed the advice to stay sweet with the wine. Grenache and sparkling Shiraz make interesting options, or for a different approach, try a fruit wine and drizzle a corresponding fruit sauce over the chocolate!

### Cheese

Try anything. It won't hurt. A wine salesperson once said, "If you want to sell wine, serve cheese." Cheese makes everything taste good. Cheese is highly recommended before dinner, during dinner, and definitely after dinner. Creamy cheese is tasty with a creamy wine like white Rhône blends, harder aged cheese sings with a solid wine like Carmenère. And a beautiful match that never goes out of style is salty blue cheese and sweet Sauternes or late-harvest wine.

## Food and Wine Pairing Tips

- Consider intensity. Big-flavoured wines tend to go with big-flavoured foods. What does "big-flavoured" mean? Full-bodied, fruit-forward wines you really feel in your mouth. The corollary is that light-flavoured wines tend to suit lighter dishes (the wild-card is sparkling wine, which seems to be able to go with just about any food thanks to its overtones of refreshment and celebration). This is the key reason why a robust Malbec runs roughshod over mixed greens but is amazing with a mixed grill.

- Either contrast or match food and wine flavours. A buttery Chardonnay matches a creamy alfredo sauce, and a meaty Cabernet matches, well, meat. On the other hand, a crisp and fruity Sauvignon Blanc works wonders in contrasting briny, rich oysters—and a fizzy, slightly sweet Lambrusco can tame a plate of fully loaded nachos.

- It's OK to play with your food. Just opened a Shiraz with an extra peppery kick? Try grinding a bit of black pepper on the dish to bridge the gap. Is that zesty Albariño overpowering the seafood? Squeeze a few drops of lemon juice on your fish to help things jive.

- Build flavour bridges. Can any wine go with any food? That's a stretch, but if your food is balanced in flavour, you stack the odds in favour of a successful match. A steak or salmon on its own is a recipe for the doldrums, but a sprinkle of salt or a bit of lime will give the food some seasoned balance. A garden salad with a handful of roasted pine or pumpkin nuts (or bacon bits!) to flesh out an acidic vinaigrette will increase the wine-pairing potential.

- Keep things in perspective. Food and wine matches are moving targets. One night's perfect match may not prove as memorable the next day or week. Context and company also go with the wine and food.

# Icon Maps

There is a wine for every meal, and there is a wine for every occasion. These icons will appear alongside each review to offer a few suggested food pairings and occasions to enjoy with every wine.

## Food Icons

**Beef**  Big protein, whether it's roast, steak, or stew

**Cheese**  Hard or soft, stinky or mild

**Dessert**  Sweet, sticky, fruity, and fun!

**Fish**  Big or small, whole or fillet

**Lamb**  The other red meat

**On its own**  'Nuff said

**Pork**  Chops, kebabs, loin—from nose to tail

**Poultry**  Turkey, chicken, duck, and any fowl

**Shellfish**  Bivalves and crustaceans

**Vegetarian**  Garden-approved and tofu-friendly

## Occasions

**BYO**  Crowd-pleasers; wines to pack along to the dinner party

**Classic**  Wines that show good typicity; varietally true bottles

**Patio/Picnic**  Sunshine in a bottle; sipping wines ready for alfresco dining

**Rock Out**  Wines to let your hair down and crank it up to 11

**Romance**  Wines to get busy with

**Wednesday Wine**  Everyday bottles to get you through the mid-week hump

**Wine Geek**  Eclectic wines outside the usual bottled domain

**Winter Warmer**  Wines to ward off any chill

 Look for this icon to occasionally appear on the neck of wine bottles. It's an indication that the wine is made from organically grown grapes.

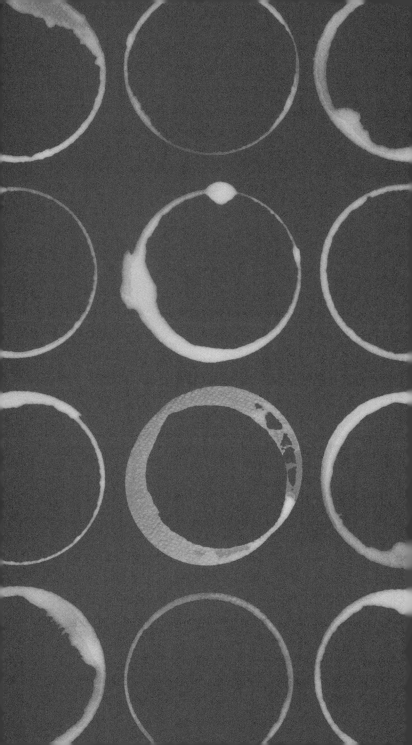

# The Whites

Hungary

# Count Károlyi

**2013 Grüner Veltliner**
**$9.29**

**A few years back, Grüner Veltliner was heralded as the next "it" white wine.** While this never really took, it's certainly worth taking a look at Count Károlyi's awesomely priced GV. It's super citrusy, with a burst of lemon and apple fruit leading to a zippy, mid-weight mouthfeel that finds a crisp, clean finish. This is a great introduction to Grüner Veltliner, which goes gaga with a bocce ball in the other hand (or a bucket of fried chicken).

GRÜNER VELTLINER

2013

DRY WHITE WINE SELECTION

COUNT KÁROLYI

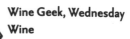 **Bacon and Brussels sprouts**

 **Fried chicken**

 **Wine Geek, Wednesday Wine**

4002301430773

Portugal

# Casal Garcia

Vinho Verde
**$10.99**

**Vinho Verde taught me the wet-newspaper-cooler technique.** This was in Rio de Janeiro, where bottles of Vinho Verde got wrapped up in newspaper, doused under the faucet, and dumped into the over-the-shoulder soft pack for the trip to one of Rio's hillside favelas. Almost two hours later, sipped out of tumblers and with million-dollar views out on the City of God, this straight-up, light, and zesty white was still refreshingly cold—and the best possible wine for the occasion.

On its own

Bacalao fritters

Patio/Picnic, Classic

5601096208308

British Columbia

# Calona Vineyards

2013 Sovereign Opal
$11.29

**Let's pause a moment for a feel-good, patriotic grape story.** Sovereign Opal is a uniquely Canadian tale. The grape, an esoteric crossing of Maréchal Foch and Golden Muscat, was developed at the Pacific Agri-Food Research Centre in Summerland. Sovereign Opal was specifically bred to be hardy enough to sustain Okanagan Valley winters while maintaining good aromatics and fruit. And it is decidedly aromatic: with great floral notes, citrus, and stone fruit, it offers significant character for the price. Fulsome depth and roundness lead to an off-dry yet still tangy and fresh finish.

Hummus and pita

Smoked turkey sandwiches

 Wine Geek, Patio/Picnic

CALONA·VINEYARDS
ARTIST SERIES

*Summer Meadow ~ Robb Dunfield*

*Sovereign Opal*
BC VQA OKANAGAN VALLEY
2013

58976400041

South Africa

# Douglas Green

**2014 Chardonnay**
**$11.29**

**Douglas Green's Chardonnay is a cheery white from South Africa that is ready (and willing) to toast a crowd.** Bright citrus and apple fruit lead to toasty, spicy oak on a soft, languid finish in this mellow style of Chardonnay that checks all the crowd-pleasing boxes. It makes for an easy solo sipper, not to mention an able partner poured with an array of dishes, from Thai takeout to cabbage rolls.

Cabbage rolls

Pad thai

Wednesday Wine, BYO

6001812011059

Chile

# Casillero del Diablo

**2014 Reserva Sauvignon Blanc**
**$12.29**

**Let me be blunt.** This bottle offers the same quality and character as most Sauvignon Blancs twice its price (or at least 1.5 times). It has the aromatics (pleasing lemon and cut grass), and it has the depth and intensity (not to mention that it's robust yet finessed). All said, it has my vote for a reliable, all-round dining companion.

RESERVA

**Casillero del Diablo**

SAUVIGNON BLANC / 2014
CHILE

CASILLERO DEL DIABLO, THE DEVIL'S

CHA Y TORO

 Roast chickpeas

 Fish and chips

 Wednesday Wine, Winter Warmer

7804320301174

# McLarens on the Lake

**2014 Unwooded Chardonnay**
**$12.29**

**This is block-party wine.** No joke: share this with the neighbours on a hot, sun-soaked summer day to stellar reviews. It's not like there's some secret to success here, it's simply a fresh, fun, and unoaked Chardonnay resounding with bright apple, peach, and flower blossom that finishes crisply. It's also a fine base for a wine spritzer, not to mention a charming partner with fish off the grill.

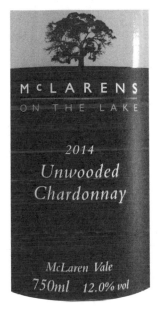

With fruit juice and soda in a spritzer

Grilled halibut tacos

Patio/Picnic, Rock Out

9329743001244

Argentina

# Santa Julia

**2014 Pinot Grigio**
**$12.29**

**Here's a solid, straight-up mid-week companion.** Fresh but round and textured, Santa Julia's Pinot Grigio hits all the wine comfort buttons: a smooth, plush entry; even more of an apple and citrus kiss; and engaging floral tones and good balance to conclude. It's just begging to be served up with those quick-and-easy mid-week meals.

Baked bean burritos

Chops in mushroom sauce

Romance, Rock Out

Argentina

# Graffigna

2014 Centenario Pinot Grigio
Reserva
$12.79

**Full disclosure: I'm predisposed to not like Pinot Grigio.**
Okay, that's too harsh. It's not that I don't like Pinot Grigio, it's more that I'm likely to walk past it on the shelves. The reason being that given how popular Pinot Grigio is these days, many examples have become, well, pretty boring and PG. But then I tasted the latest vintage of Graffigna Grigio, and then I checked the price, and it certainly offered great pear and floral notes, not to mention a fruity approach and crisp finish. In short, it's a modern, honest Pinot Grigio ready to tackle everyday wine-pairing duties.

 Chef salad

Lemon chicken

 Wednesday Wine, BYO

South Africa

# The Royal

**2013 Old Vines Chenin Blanc
$12.79**

**"And we'll never be royals (royals)..."** Sorry, but every time I glance at the label of this awesome-value Chenin Blanc, Lorde's resounding voice reverberates through my glass. It's true, at least in my case, but nonetheless I certainly feel royal spending a non-princely sum to get this lush and honeyed white in my glass. Tropical fruit and baked apple abound in this fruity, off-dry Chenin Blanc that is juicy and downright intense. It's quite rich through to a lengthy finish, making it a great solo sipper as well as a partner for grilled chicken.

On its own

Grilled lemongrass chicken

Rock Out, Wine Geek

784585012169

France

# Le Paradou

2014 Viognier
$12.99

**Here's a change from the wine norm.** It has all the floral potpourri and tropical fruit one wants in a Viognier, including a super-fruity mid-palate. But underneath the explosive aromatics, there is elegance and allure, with a perfumed mid-palate segueing to a fresh finish, signalling this wine's multitasking food-pairing prowess.

 Taleggio

 Mushrooms on toast

 Romance, Winter Warmer

2014

## LE PARADOU
### Viognier

On pourrait croire que le mot Paradou signifie Paradis dans la langue d'oc, tant il fait bon vivre chez nous, dans le sud de la France. Pourtant il signifie en réalité «Moulin». C'est en hommage à ces géants majestueux, bâtis sur les berges des cours d'eau depuis les temps Romains, et aujourd'hui pour la plupart endormis, que nous avons créé ces vins de fraîcheur et de plaisir.

626990005377

Italy

# Castello Monaci

### 2013 Acante Fiano
### $13.29

**Fun-loving Fiano.** Say that 10 times fast. Castello Monaci's Acante Fiano hails from Salento, the southeastern "heel" of Italy's proverbial geographic "boot," and it checks in at a very respectable (and refined) alcohol level of 12%. But don't get fooled by the modest alcohol by volume (ABV), this fun white still brings serious flavour. It's lighter-bodied but certainly not shy, with bright citrus and honeyed notes. All said, it's tough to hate on a fresh, easygoing, and easy-to-pair white that will work with everything from pork carnitas to baked salmon.

 Baked salmon

Carnitas tacos

Classic, Wednesday Wine

8000160673719

Spain

# El Petit Bonhomme

**2013 Blanco**
**$13.29**

**Perfume and presence.** Come to think of it, that's a pretty catchy name for an aromatherapy retail outlet. Actually, though, they are the two traits that caught my attention in this pleasing, pleasantly priced white. Hailing from the Rueda region of Spain where the Verdejo grape reigns, El Petit Bonhomme consistently delivers an enticing mix of lemony fruit and a savoury, herbal core. Thus, it's juicy and mouth-filling but also perfumed and crisp, a fine all-around combination that culminates in presence and grace.

On its own

Pea pesto

BYO, Patio/Picnic

8437012278264

France

# Moillard

### 2013 Hugues le Juste Viognier
### $13.29

**"Enjoy now while fresh."** This is the advice proffered on the back label of this spritely white, and I wish more wineries would be so forthcoming. The reality is that the bulk of white wines (and, yes, the same goes for reds) are not meant for the cellar. Perhaps it would be more useful to include a "best before" date on bottles for encouragement? Anyways, grab a bottle of Hugues le Juste Viognier and crack its screw cap pronto in order to get the most of its enticing apricot and rosewater aromatics. It's quite smooth overall, with a lingering plush yet fresh finish.

On its own

Barbequed oysters

Patio/Picnic, Rock Out

Germany

# Landlust

2013 Riesling
$13.99

**Aside from the bicycle label, I dig this wine.** Don't get me wrong, I'm a big fan of two-wheeled transportation. I've even been known to commute by bike when possible. But there seems to be this notion that anything bike-related is hip, happening, and "green." Sure, I appreciate that this friendly Riesling is made from organically grown Mosel vineyard grapes. But I appreciate the gregarious peach and apple and fresh, easygoing style of this off-dry Riesling even more. So gather up your bike courier friends, grill up some currywurst, and you're set!

**Organically Grown**

 **Currywurst**

 **Tofu tacos**

**Patio/Picnic, Romance**

4003301064067

Argentina

# Crios de Susana Balbo

2014 Torrontés
$14.49

**Tasting this wine always makes me think about having my mouth washed out with soap.** But in a wonderful way that's just for grown-ups. Impossibly floral, gushing rose petal and orange blossom, its engaging aromatics are offset by a rich, lush texture and smooth, fresh finish. This unoaked white would pair wonderfully with grilled chicken or fish, but it's also splendid for solo sipping.

On its own

Bruschetta

Wine Geek, Patio/Picnic

7798068480300

United States

# Chateau Ste. Michelle

2014 Riesling
$14.79

**A winter warming wine doesn't automatically mean red.** There's nothing like fondue to feed the stomach and the soul on a cold winter's night, and I'd much rather pair the cheesy goodness with a robust white in my wineglass. Riesling makes a great match with the fondue pot, and Chateau Ste. Michelle's Columbia Valley–sourced bottling offers lush peach and pear fruit balanced by a crisp, citrusy finish. It's warming yet refreshing at the same time.

 Fondue

 Roast with crackling

 Winter Warmer, Rock Out

88586621840

Italy

# Lagaria

**2013 Pinot Grigio**
**$14.79**

**Admittedly, the label is a tad too much.** All fashion-forward and scenester-ish, digitally animated scooter included. Whatever—look past it. Get off your moped high horse, or simply turn the page, because the wine inside is classic Italian Pinot Grigio. Lagaria offers classy citrus aromas in a crisp, modern white that oozes fun fruit while maintaining a classic, grapey finish.

On its own

Cod fritters

Patio/Picnic, BYO

726452001173

New Zealand

# Marisco Vineyards

**2014 The Ned Sauvignon Blanc**
**$14.79**

**These days there's a tendency to want to stand out.** Individualism has run amok. It's all well and good, but just remember that being an individual does not equate to having character. Indeed, often those who don't attempt to stand out ultimately shine through with the most character. Same goes for wine. Too many Sauvignon Blancs get all aggro on the taste buds in an attempt to impress; however, The Ned—while certainly zippy and fruity and everything you would want in a New Zealand Sauv Blanc—massages the palate with elegant aromatics, mid-palate finesse, and a balanced finish.

 On its own

Veggie tempura

Wednesday Wine, Patio/ Picnic

9421901182038

British Columbia

# Red Rooster

**2014 Gewürztraminer**
**$14.79**

**Gewürztraminer likes to get the party started.** At least, if grapes had personalities, you'd be hard-pressed to find a more exuberant, outgoing cultivar. Check out Red Rooster's Gew to see what this all means. A cornucopia of classic orange peel, tropical fruit, and rose-water aromas lead off in this fruity, off-dry Gewürztraminer that builds to a bold, slightly spicy finish.

 Chicken stir-fry

 BLT sandwiches

 Wednesday Wine, Rock Out

681246800199

Germany

# Über

2013 Riesling Kabinett
$14.79

**It's the wine Über,**
Not the liquid car service,
Easy, peachy, fresh.

 On its own

 Prawn curry

 Winter Warmer, Classic

785859876814

Chile

# Casas del Bosque

**2012 Reserva Sauvignon Blanc
$14.99**

**Whammo!** This is all-in, intense Sauvignon Blanc. Outsized citrus, tropical fruit, and mineral notes set the stage for this rich yet nicely balanced Sauvignon Blanc that hails from the westernmost reaches of Chile's renowned cool-climate Casablanca Valley. Yes, it's fresh and zippy, but it also ends with a clean, fruity, and approachable finish.

Catfish po'boy

Oyster po'boy

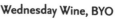 Wednesday Wine, BYO

# Hester Creek

2014 Pinot Blanc
$14.99

**Locally, Pinot Gris gets most of the press for the white Pinot family.** As the singular red, Pinot Noir has always earned its fair share of fame. That leaves Pinot Blanc as the odd Pinot out. We don't hear that much about Pinot Blanc, which is a shame because it also takes well to British Columbia's vineyards. Case in point is long-running winery Hester Creek's juicy PB, which oozes peachy-apricot goodness and goes down mighty easy.

Sautéed trout

Veggie burgers

Patio/Picnic, Romance

626037001126

**Organically Grown**

Portugal

# Quinta do Ameal

*2013 Loureiro Vinho Verde*
*$15.29*

**Vinho Verde literally translates from Portuguese as "green wine."** However, it is more usefully associated as "young wine," for while many Vinho Verdes are slightly spritzy and exuberantly tangy in their near-underripe state, not all VVs are singularly focused on maximum refreshment for minimum investment. Quinta do Ameal's Vinho Verde, for example, is much more. Sure, it's vibrant and refreshing, but it's also intense, with layers of complex citrus, floral, and mineral tones. That said, it is—*ahem*—green in the sense that it is made from organically grown Loureiro grapes indigenous to the Minho province of Portugal.

 Mussels

Chicken tenders with plum sauce

 Wine Geek, Romance

5604882989108

Austria

# Domäne Wachau

**2012 Terraces Grüner Veltliner**
**$15.79**

**Herein I submit Exhibit A for most sass in a wine bottle.** A fantastic, fresh Grüner Veltliner hailing from the terrace-lined banks of the Danube River in the Wachau region of Austria, this white certainly brings it—the "it" being zippy citrus, apple, and mineral notes in a wine that would merely be posing if its crispness weren't matched by its depth and complexity. To conclude: there's a little spice, a little honeyed fruit, and a smooth, balanced finish. So not only does it have some cheekiness, but it also has the sumptuous mouthfeel to back it all up.

Smoked mozzarella

Unagi Don

Winter Warmer, BYO

9007500050987

Germany

## Selbach

**2013 Riesling**
**$15.79**

**This is a perennial go-to pick.**
Year in and year out, you can
count on Selbach to deliver the
Riesling goods. Which is all
about generous apple, flower
blossom, and honey notes in an
off-dry package. It's tangy overall, proving that there can
indeed be harmony and balance
between residual sugars and
acidity. More baked apple and
fizzy grape candies lead to a
fresh and fruity finish. Simply
put, this is a great all-round
Riesling and everyday food
partner.

Gouda grilled cheese

Baked chicken strips

Wednesday Wine,
Classic

717215001707

Spain

# Luzada

2013 Albariño
$15.99

**Where has all the Albariño gone?** Some years back, it felt like this grape was about to hit the big time, become the new Sauvignon Blanc. This was largely thanks to the bracing Albariño from northwest Spain. But alas, it was not to be, and Sauvignon Blanc became the new, well, Sauvignon Blanc. Thus it was all the more exciting to find a new awesomely priced Albariño from Spain's Rias Baixas, which rekindles the romance for these tangy, floral, and citrus-packed whites. The Luzada is juicy and super crisp, and the perfect pick when seafood is on your plate.

 New England clam chowder

Trout Almondine

 Wine Geek, Rock Out

8437008356150

France

# Domaine Roc de Châteauvieux

**2013 Touraine**
**$16.49**

**It's old-school Sauvignon Blanc with new-school appeal!** With all the hype surrounding New World Sauv Blanc from the likes of New Zealand, Chile, and British Columbia, it can be easy to forget that the grape got its start in France. The "wild white" is purportedly indigenous to southwest France and continues to be an important variety in both Bordeaux and the Loire. The latter features in this citrusy, herbaceous Touraine, which is dry and fresh throughout and concludes with a serious zippiness.

On its own

Oysters on the half-shell

Rock Out, Romance

3245370423036

France

# Kuhlmann-Platz

2013 Gewürztraminer
$16.49

**One-word wine review: sumptuous.** Classic Gewürztraminer is all about Northern European vineyards. If you're used to drinking New World Gewürztraminer, Alsace's Kuhlmann-Platz offers another fun take on this aromatic grape. On first sniff, aromas abound: lifted rose petal notes, stone fruit, and super lychee. A soft, fruity entry marks this as a crowd-pleaser, with a honeyed mouthfeel leading to an off-dry—albeit fresh and balanced—finish. It's great to taste side by side with a homegrown B.C. version, all in the name of wine education, of course!

On its own

Baked halibut

Winter Warmer, Rock Out

3306997130704

British Columbia

# Wild Goose

**2014 Autumn Gold**
**$16.59**

**Here's a B.C. standby.** Each year, Wild Goose's Autumn gold arrives to provide fruity fun in wineglasses. Not quite Gold in colour, this blend of equal parts Riesling, Gewürztraminer, and Pinot Blanc offers great aromas of stone fruit, pear, and citrus. Off-dry and soft, it concludes with good freshness and a lip-smacking finish. It's the kind of wine that can't help but put a smile on your face as you sip.

On its own

Chicken korma

Wednesday Wine, BYO

626990007296

Italy

# Miopasso

### 2012 Fiano
### $16.79

**Fiano is freaking fantastic!** An ancient grape found throughout southern Italy, Fiano has re-emerged as an enticing, intriguing white capable of tasty food-pairing prowess. See what the fuss is all about with Miopasso's Fiano, which hails from the Gela area in eastern Sicily and provides classic floral, pear, and citrus pith nuances. It comes across fruity but also savoury, with engaging depth and a boisterous, juicy finish.

 Porchetta sandwich

Pea and lemon risotto

Patio/Picnic, Wine Geek

8034115191270

New Zealand

# Babich

### 2014 Sauvignon Blanc
### $17.39

**Fresh but elegant, overt yet restrained.** Babich's Sauvignon Blanc deftly walks the tightrope, providing a great middle-of-the-road style of smooth, ripe gooseberry and tropical fruit complemented by a twang of crispness. The end result is a crowd-pleasing, fun, and fresh white with multi-tasking food-pairing opportunities, from sun-dried tomato and goat cheese tart to smoked trout.

Young chèvre

Smoked trout

Classic, Patio/Picnic

9414603201107

France

# Pfaffenheim

2013 Pfaff Pinot Gris
$17.49

**This is a plush counterpoint to all those prissy, crisp Pinot Grigios.** The classic Pfaff Pinot Gris looks serious in the glass from the get-go, all bright golden and dense. Aromas of tropical fruit and citrus lead off in this lush, smooth, and honeyed white that is unabashedly rich. Evident residual sugars await, but this bold white features engaging spice and a smooth finish as counterbalancing flavour measures.

 On its own

Schnitzel

Classic, Winter Warmer

3185130071025

Australia

# Wakefield

### 2014 Riesling
### $17.49

**Seriously, if you haven't tasted an Australian Riesling, go buy this bottle.** Generally, they tend to be unlike any other Rieslings. In fact, it's a style represented wonderfully by this bottle of Wakefield Riesling. Pouring a bright, light golden in the glass, it seems straightforward enough until first sip. Suddenly, the taste buds are met with super-intense, tangy sensations of citrus and apple blossom—before they pucker up for the zesty, quite dry finish.

Aged cheddar

Shrimp pasta alfresco

Classic, Rock Out

9311659000527

South Africa

# DeMorgenzon

**2013 DMZ Chardonnay**
**$17.79**

**Everything about this South African Chardonnay screams class.** From the stylish label with old-school flair to the rich and creamy contents within, this elegant Chard impresses. Aromas of citrus, tropical fruit, and vanilla lead off in this full-bodied white, with barrel fermentation imbuing layers of flavour and a sumptuous texture before a bright, bold, but nicely balanced finish.

On its own

Thai lemongrass chicken sausages

Romance, Wine Geek

6009820750328

Italy

# Umani Ronchi

**2013 CaSal di Serra Verdicchio Classico Superiore**
**$17.99**

**The name is a tongue twister, but the wine is a total palate pleaser.** The full name is Umani Ronchi CaSal di Serra Verdicchio dei Castelli di Jesi Classico Superiore, but you can call it "killer Verdicchio" for short. Featuring fresh intensity with an elegant kiss of citrus, this succulent white expresses power without sacrificing balance—it's a great option for white wine enthusiasts looking to break away from the norm.

 Poached halibut

Lasagna

Wine Geek, Romance

8032853721124

# Robert Mondavi Winery

**2013 Fumé Blanc**
**$18.79**

**"A dry Sauvignon Blanc."** This statement is printed front and centre across Mondavi's Fumé Blanc label. It's a helpful issuance, and I can attest to the wine's dry finish. Of course, while quoting labels it's also worth noting that "Robert Mondavi created the first Fumé Blanc in 1966." While at the time I'm sure this had marketing gravitas, today most people are like, "What's a Fumé Blanc?" Well, it's Sauvignon Blanc, and in this case it has citrus and floral aromatics alongside a fresh but robust entry and a citrusy—and, yes, dry—finish.

**Greek salad**

**Turkey scallopini**

**Patio/Picnic, BYO**

86003351868

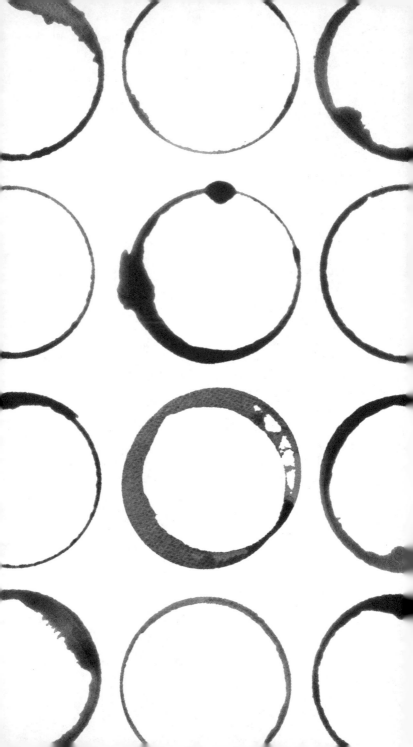

# The Rosés

Chile

# Cono Sur

**2014 Bicicleta Pinot Noir Rosé**
**$9.79**

**Crowd-pleasing rosé for a tenner?** Might as well grab a case. Cono Sur heads to the Bío-Bío Valley in Chile's southern realms to source Pinot Noir grapes for its super-juicy, super-aromatic rosé. Pouring an engaging pink with orange highlights, it's rich yet tart up front—and outsized overall—with a fresh and fruity stature that screams "Make me your friend." This is picnic wine; it's great served family-style, whether turkey sandwiches or grilled ribs are on the menu.

Turkey sandwiches

Sauce-slathered ribs

BYO, Patio/Picnic

Spain

# Olivares

2014 Jumilla Rosado
$11.29

**This is everyday drinking rosé.**
Or Rosado, to be precise, considering this light pink wine originates from Spain. The grape makeup has changed over the years, with the latest vintage featuring a workaday blend of 70% Garnacha and 30% Monastrell. It offers up a fruity entry of berry and cherry candy before settling into a lighter-bodied mouthfeel overall and a zesty finish to end. It's straightforward, straight up, and ready to pair with anything off the grill, or even a nice rose-coloured sunset.

 On its own

Grilled chops

 Wednesday Wine, Romance

8437001433148

Argentina

# Amaru

**2015 High Vineyard Torrontés Rosé**
**$13.99**

**Rosé made from Torrontés, say what?** Isn't Torrontés a white grape? Why, yes indeed, but Amaru cold-soaks 95% Torrontés and 5% Malbec on skins to achieve this clear, pale pink beauty that holds forth with peach blossom and gummy candies. It's a neat idea that showcases Argentina's two darling grapes, and it's super-fresh and super-fun sipping. A fruity, slightly off-dry finish makes this a good option for somewhat spicy foods, or just serve with the bocce game and be done.

On its own

Thai tofu curry

Patio/Picnic, Wine Geek

7790189041910

Australia

# Angove Family Winemakers

**2014 Nine Vines Grenache Shiraz Rosé**
**$14.49**

**We are amidst a rosé revolution.** I see it on the shelves; it's evidenced amongst the pages of Had a Glass; heck, even casual conversations (not to mention wine-buying statistics) point to more and more pink wine being available and consumed. This is a good trend because not only does rosé tend to be fun, it also tends to partner well with a myriad of cuisine. Angove's Grenach Shiraz Rosé lands squarely on the fun side, with its cool neon pink colour leading to rhubarb and currant aromas and a fresh finish with good balance. It's simple, it's fun, and it's one more reason to drink pink.

 Fish masala

Vietnamese shredded pork

Rock Out, Wednesday Wine

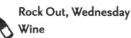

650814000477

THE ROSÉS | 91

British Columbia

# Quails' Gate

**2014 Rosé**
**$15.69**

**Everyone who tastes this rosé loves it.** Which is why it returns for another year. It's become the go-to local pink wine pick for my friends and neighbours, which is saying something. Every year, Quails' Gate delivers with tasty aplomb. This year's rosé is a gregarious blend of mostly Gamay Noir with Pinot Noir and Pinot Gris (80%/10%/10%), cold-soaked on skins for a few hours to extract flavour and a gorgeous deep pink colour. Lots of berry flavours mingle with earthy notes in this pink quaffer.

Chicken quesadilla

Chinese-style jellyfish

Patio/Picnic, Classic

777885610624 4

France

# Bieler Père et Fils

2014 Coteaux d'Aix-en-Provence
Rosé
$15.79

**Great value from the heartland of rosé!** Did you know that there are three demarcated wine appellations in Provence, which is itself the largest rosé-producing wine region in the world? The largest is Côtes de Provence, the smallest is Coteaux Varois, and the farthest west is Coteaux d'Aix-en-Provence. This appellation abuts the Rhône Valley and is known for its Mistral wind, which keeps rain at bay while also infusing a cold, dry air. It's home to this bottle of Bieler Père et Fils, which pours a pale, pale pink and comes across savoury with aromas of herbs and apple skin followed by a dryly tart and tangy finish that doesn't obscure the wine's delicateness.

 Quiche

Sautéed shrimp

Patio/Picnic, Romance

856622001013

Spain

# Muga

**2014 Rioja Rosado**
**$15.79**

**This is real-deal rosé (or Rosado, as they say in Spain).** Muga's enticing pink wine hails from the famed Rioja region of Spain, where it's crafted from the typical local grapes Garnacha, Viura, and Tempranillo. Don't be fooled by its pale pink colour, this rosé is all power up front with serious intensity and depth complemented by notes of stone fruit and dusty earth. It's fulsome and full-on ready to serve with hearty fare: we're talking roast lamb leg or barbequed ribs.

Ribs

Roast leg

Wednesday Wine, BYO

British Columbia

# Clos du Soleil

**2014 Rosé**
**$17.29**

**This is the year for homegrown rosé!** Actually, the recent trend has been an influx of local pink wine, a movement that I am happy to support. We have the geography to craft exciting rosé, and local punters are proving they have a thirst for pink, so it makes sense. Clos du Soleil opts for Cabernet Sauvignon in producing their bright pink, exuberant berry-enhanced rosé. It has great depth and richness, not to mention it goes down easy thanks to a round, lingering balanced finish.

On its own

Cuban sandwiches

Rock Out, Patio/Picnic

857088000565

British Columbia

# Joie

**2014 Rosé**
**$18.99**

**"Re-Think Pink."** Naramata-based Joie Farm makes a rosé call to arms with this label-emblazoned urge for wine drinkers. And a glass of their zippy, super-refreshing style of rosé may very well beckon punters over to the pink wine side. Pouring a bright pink, it invites with aromas of candied watermelon before a tart finish, traits that give this pink wine extreme food-pairing savviness. Anything with a little smoke and char will work well with this rosé, from grilled marinated tofu to balsamic-glazed grilled chicken.

Grilled extra firm tofu

Balsamic-glazed chicken

Patio/Picnic, Romance

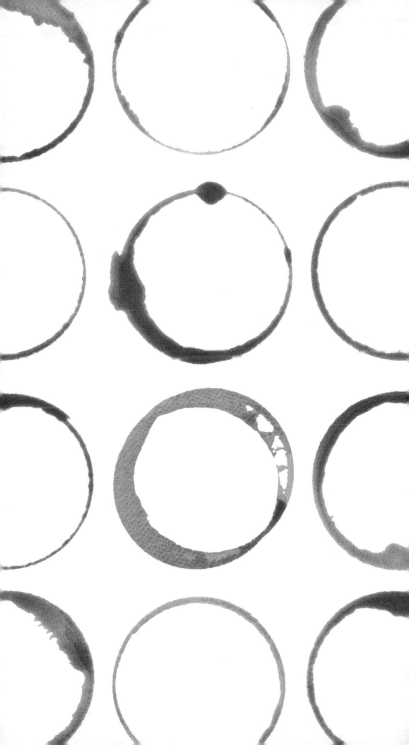

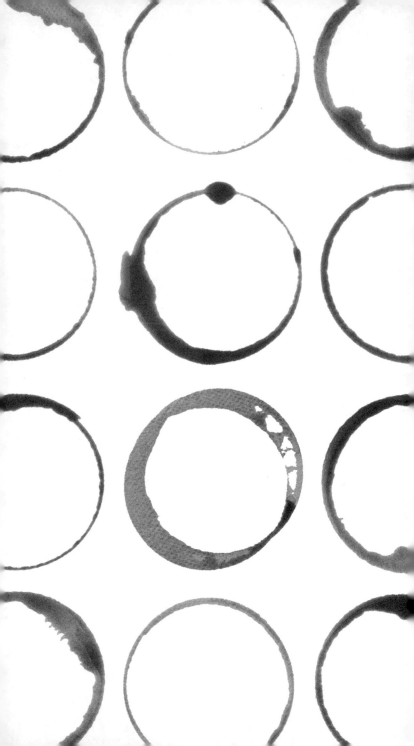

# The Reds

# Periquita

2013 Original
$8.79

**Started from the bottom, now
we're here.** You know, I used to
buy Periquita when I was a uni-
versity student because it was
one of the only wines I could
afford. Now, I still buy Periquita
because it's a darn fine everyday
red that offers a heck of a lot of
character for under 10 bucks.
Credit the trio of grapes working together in this Portuguese
mix (Castelão, Trincadeira, and
Aragonez), which creates a plush
yet vibrant overall style that
matches up with a myriad of
daily plates, from cheese-filled
ravioli to meat loaf.

Spinach ricotta ravioli

Meat loaf

Wednesday Wine, Classic

5601174204000

Chile

# Santa Rita

2013 "120" Merlot
$9.59

**This wine has guts for the price.** Predominant aromas of currant and blackberry introduce this juicy, fruit-forward Merlot that continues to exude vanilla and ripe fruit through the mid-palate. That said, it finishes fresh with toasty, spicy oak and overall good balance, making it a great pick for those budget-conscious days. Pair with hearty stews or braised dishes.

 Tagine

 Braised tofu

 Wednesday Wine, Rock Out

7804330211203

Bulgaria

# Lovico

### 2011 Gamza
### $9.99

**Go, Gamza, go!** Just kidding, as that meme is reserved for Gamay (#goGamaygo, anyone?), but for fans of lesser-appreciated grapes, it's worth checking out this fun and unique bottle. An important and popular dark-skinned grape used widely throughout Eastern Europe, Lovico's Gamza offers aromas of black cherry and sunbaked earth in an overall supple, velvety style with a smooth but short finish. It's a great wine to bring to your wine-know-it-all friend's house.

 On its own

Bulgarian stew

 Wine Geek, BYO

Portugal

# Casa Ermelinda Freitas

2012 Monte da Baía Tinto
$11.29

**South of Lisbon, across the River Tagus, lies the Setúbal Peninsula.** This mostly flat, sandy region has been sending over a slew of nicely priced Portuguese reds, including the grippy, intriguing Monte da Baía. A rich entry is offset by mineral notes and some bell pepper, building to a lengthy finish with good intensity. In short, it's gutsy but poised—perfect with robust, comforting meals such as ratatouille and braised lamb.

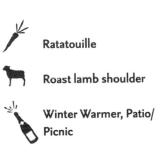

Ratatouille

Roast lamb shoulder

Winter Warmer, Patio/Picnic

5608527002054

France

# Paul Mas

**2013 Grenache Noir**
**$11.29**

**This is the wine equivalent of "Dad Bod."** Soft and friendly through and through, this Grenache from the south of France squishes and cuddles the taste buds more than anything else. Which is not a bad thing by any means, unless you prefer chiselled, hard-edged fruit and acidity to sweet and ripe berry coddled by endearing lifted bramble and spice. Anyways, who needs six-packs when there's a wineglass, right?

Pepperoni pizza

Duck prosciutto

Romance, Rock Out

France

# Cave Saint Desirat

2012 Syrah
$11.49

**Here's proof that Syrah doesn't have to rely on overly ripe fruit or abundantly high alcohol to pack a punch.** Saint Desirat manages to arrive in the glass with a mélange of concentrated berry fruit and savoury aromatics while sporting 12% ABV and an approachable price tag. It's an estate-bottled red crafted from hand-harvested grapes grown in the Saint-Joseph region of the northern Rhône, and it goes gangbusters with Chinese roast duck or grilled venison sausages.

Roast duck

Grilled sausages

 BYO, Rock Out

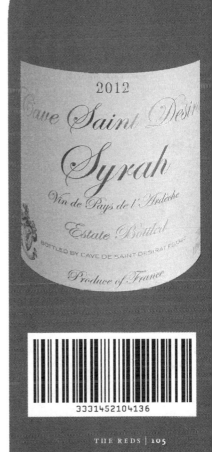

3331452104136

 Montenegro

# Plantaže

2010 Vranac
$11.79

**Time for a bit of grape trivia to stump your dinner guests.** What is the most important grape variety in Montenegro? Why, Vranac, of course, which is both a grape and a brand of wine in this Adriatic Sea–fronting nation. Better yet, after you've quizzed your dining companions, open a bottle of Plantaže Vranac for a taste. It has a pleasant fruity approach, with crushed flower petal, herbs, and berry. Vibrant overall and very dry to finish, this wine also has a tart spiciness that makes it both engaging and easy-sipping.

Spanish rice-stuffed peppers

Stew

Wine Geek, BYO

Spain

# Castillo de Almansa

**2011 Riserva**
**$12.29**

**It's time to tuck the taste buds in for the night.** Or at least a night of wining, as Castillo de Almansa's sumptuous Riserva will have them cozying up to the wineglass. After spending 12 months in American oak, this blend of Tempranillo, Monastrell, and Garnacha further rests in bottle before being shipped from south-central Spain to all parts of the globe. Ripe black cherry and the oomph of toasty oak come together in this juicy, yet dry and structured, nicely priced bottle.

 Cana de Oveja

Braised shanks

Wednesday Wine, Winter Warmer

Chile

# Santa Carolina

**2013 Reserva Pinot Noir**
**$12.29**

**It's Pinot Noir for the paupers!**
Exaggeration to be sure, it's just that Pinot Noir has a reputation for being pricey. And while no doubt the finest Burgundies and other examples of archetypal Pinot Noir cost a pretty penny, the 99% of us can still have fun with Pinot Noir. Santa Carolina's wallet-friendly PN is modern in style, with aggressive berry and forest-floor aromatics matched with juicy fruit and a plush finish. It's not the most complicated Pinot Noir, but it's certainly attractive, and it over-delivers for the price.

On its own

Jerky

Wednesday Wine, Patio/
Picnic

Argentina

# Alamos

2013 Cabernet Sauvignon
$13.29

**Bottle got back!** With apologies to Sir Mix-A-Lot (Pacific Northwest, represent!), this is straight-up good posture wine. It's a Cabernet Sauvignon with poise, deftly balancing its ripe dark fruit and toasty oak and tobacco leaf with delicate floral tones and overall flavour finesse. In short, it's bold but elegant, making this red a great everyday food partner, from roast pork to grilled lamb.

Braised shoulder

Grilled lamb shoulder
Provençale

Classic, Wednesday Wine

South Africa

# Boekenhoutskloof

**2014 The Wolftrap Red**
**$13.29**

**This is an easy pick when
people tell me they want a bold
red at a not-so-beaucoup price.**
A gutsy blend of Syrah,
Mourvèdre, and Viognier, this
South African fruit-bomb manages to bring dark fruit, leather,
and herbs into a flamboyant yet
sumptuous mix. There's some
spice and grip on an otherwise
well-balanced finish; just make
sure to pair this bottle up with
some equally bold dishes, say,
achiote-rubbed pork or beef
with chimichurri.

THE WOLFTRAP

SYRAH
MOURVÈDRE VIOGNIER
RED WINE / VIN ROUGE
2013
BOEKENHOUTSKLOOF
MAIN ROAD, FRANSCHHOEK

746925000564

 Cochinita pibil

Grilled flank steak with
chimichurri

 Romance, Patio/Picnic

# Grilos

**2012 Tondela**
**$13.29**

**Grilos means "crickets" in Portuguese.** However, I suppose I'm losing something in cultural translation. For while the back label handily advises to "Let Grilos bring joy and good fortune to your table," I'm still lost on the idea of pairing wine and crickets. Anyways, the bottle is cute. Most importantly, however, the wine inside is rich and rollicking. With ripe dark fruit and toasty oak notes, it impressively manages to be robust without the flab, bringing bold flavour grafted to a punchy finish.

 Pot of stew

Lasagna

Winter Warmer, Wine Geek

Australia

# Bleasdale

**2012 Second Innings Malbec**
**$13.99**

**It's not like Argentina has a monopoly on Malbec.** The grape is used in varietal wines and as a backbone of blended wines the world over. Take Australia's Bleasdale as one example: they use 100% Langhorne Creek–sourced Malbec to produce their extremely quaffable (not to mention affordable) Second Innings Malbec. It's Malbec with a South Australian accent, full of luscious blueberry and vanilla aromas. Silky and sumptuous, this robust red comes across like liquid velvet until a dry, punchy, and spicy finish smacks the taste buds.

 On its own

 Maui ribs

 Winter Warmer, Wine Geek

Spain

# Laya

2013 Old Vines Almansa
$13.99

**"Ease of consumption."** I like this turn of phrase presented on Laya's back label. It sums things up nicely. Yes, this blend of Garnacha and Monastrell goes down rather easy, after explosive aromas of crushed berry and spice set the stage. The end result is a bold wine that still manages a light touch, that is until the somewhat-brooding and spicy conclusion (thanks, Monastrell grape!); a solid, robust all-round red.

Chorizo

Ropa vieja burritos

Wednesday Wine, Rock Out

8437005068889

France

# Les Dauphins

**2013 Côtes du Rhône Reserve**
**$13.99**

**Côtes du Rhône can be one of the most distinctive wines.** Just one whiff from a glass of CdR can be transportive: the nostrils fill with berry fruit, windswept fields of herbs, and sunbaked earth. It's all there in this bottle of Les Dauphins, which is quite remarkable given the price. Lifted aromatics, a dry and balanced disposition throughout, and a crackle of peppery spice on the finish—the potable equivalent of a pot of stew, it's comfort Côtes du Rhône.

Saint-Félicien

Stew

Classic, Wednesday Wine

3179077470195

Chile

# Undurraga

**2013 Sibaris Gran Reserva
Carménère**
**$13.99**

**The colour alone is intoxicating.** A bright dark garnet, it dazzles the eye and awakens the senses for more to come. That more is a compendium of toasty oak, ripe berry, and herby aromas that segues into a juicy approach. But this bottle is no fruit-forward flimsy; a backbone of acidity and biting spice hold things in check and ultimately help distinguish this Carménère as providing big flavour at a small price.

 On its own

 Grilled flatiron steak

Patio/Picnic, Rock Out

Argentina

# Viña Chela

**2013 Malbec Reserve**
**$13.99**

**Crowd-friendly, made from certified organically grown grapes, high-altitude sourced.** Viña Chela hits the Malbec super trifecta! Ample ripe dark fruit and toasty oak are complemented by an umami-laden savouriness in this bold, mouth-filling red. There's a lot going on for a wine of this price, which is ready to sidle up to any hearty, filling meal.

Organically
Grown

VIÑA CHELA

RESERVE

ORGANIC WINE
VIN BIOLOGIQUE

MALBEC

ARGENTINA
2013

7790415130562

Merguez sausage
sandwich

Chicken quesadilla

 Wednesday Wine, BYO

Australia

# Little Yering

2013 Pinot Noir
$14.49

**It's love at first sniff with Little Yering's Pinot Noir.** Wonderful aromatics of crushed berry and eucalyptus waft out of the glass from this bright ruby-coloured Pinot Noir from Australia's cooler-climate Yarra Valley in Victoria. It's unabashedly modern and fruit-forward yet refined and finishes dry with a tinge of spice.

 Stewed Korean pork belly

Grilled salmon

 Romance, Rock Out

659284000581

South Africa

# Painted Wolf

### 2012 The Den Pinotage
### $14.49

**This is a rather polished Pinotage.** Is this good or bad? It really depends on your stance on the grape. Pinotage purists might fret that it strays from the gritty, downright savouriness often attributed to the wine. That said, these same qualities often had punters bypassing Pinotage for Malbec et al. The Den still has guts (those herbs and dark fruit, not to mention a mouth-puckering herbiness to finish), but it also has a juicy and plush entry. Credit the grape destalking before pressing, the partial open-top fermentation, or the 10% Shiraz in the final blend—then serve this red up with fajitas or lamb palak.

Fajitas

Palak dosa

Wine Geek, Winter Warmer

# Castiglioni

2013 Chianti
$14.99

**Honest Chianti without the fluff.** Nothing more and nothing less. Like the little black dress or the perfect pair of jeans, the basics stay in style simply because they work. This straightforward Chianti does the same: it holds forth with classic black cherry, herbs, and toasty oak — the wine's fruit fended off by a savoury stance. It's smooth and balanced yet a touch brash, with evident acidity reminding us that, yes, this is how honest Sangiovese from Chianti is meant to be.

Margherita pizza

Roast rack

Classic, Patio/Picnic

8007425003649

Greece

# Boutari

2010 Naoussa
$15.79

**If you care about pairing food and wine, you should be looking for refreshing reds such as this Naoussa.** It's a cool bottle from northern Greece made with the Xinomavro grape, and it trades rich and extracted for punchy and savoury. This makes it super-versatile in the kitchen and ready to take on everything from big protein to creamy sauces.

Souvlaki

Eggplant gratin

Wine Geek, Winter Warmer

France

# M. Chapoutier Les Vignes de Bila–Haut

2012 Bila Haut
$15.79

**The first time that I tasted this wine was an eye-opener.** The tasting occurred at Chapoutier's Rhône Valley winery. It wasn't a formal tasting or anything, just a self-propelled wine tour when Bila Haut caught my eye. I think it was the reasonable 5 euro price tag! Man, did it pack a punch for the price, and though time, exchange rates, and taxes conspire to raise the price, there's no denying that this bombastic blend of Syrah, Grenache, and Carignan from southern France wallops the taste buds with ripe plum, leather, and pepper before ending with a dry, sort of savoury finish.

Burritos

Braised shank

Rock Out, Romance

Organically Grown

2011

LES VIGNES DE
BILA-HAUT

CÔTES DU ROUSSILLON VILLAGES
APPELLATION CÔTES DU ROUSSILLON VILLAGES CONTRÔLÉE

M.CHAPOUTIER
FAC ET SPERA

3391181410236

Australia

# Yalumba

**2012 Organic Shiraz**
**$15.99**

**"Vegan and vegetarian friendly."** This important distinction is helpfully provided on the back label of Yalumba's Organic Shiraz. The point being that sometimes animal-derived or -produced matter is used during the winemaking process. Not cool for vegans or vegetarians. So everyone can enjoy the enticing dark berry, anise, and Dr Pepper aromatics in this plush, elegantly balanced Shiraz. It's fruity but with an intriguing savoury underlay, with a finish flecked with peppercorns.

Grilled tofu satay

Grilled porterhouse

 Rock Out, Patio/Picnic

Organically Grown

YALUMBA
Australia's oldest family owned winery

ORGANIC WINE - VIN ORGANIQUE

Shiraz
South Australia
2012
750mL 14.1% alc./vol.

9311789001692

# Beni di Batasiolo Langhe Rosso

2012 Langhe Rosso
$16.29

**Have you heard about the lumberjack who walks into a room full of flowers?** Well, that's Langhe Rosso, which spews dark fruit and wood spice yet can't also help but bequeath a pungent floral perfume. An exuberant blend of Dolcetto, Barbera, and Nebbiolo from northern Italy, this red walks the fine line of rugged elegance, with nicely integrated flavours and a solid yet refined, elegant finish.

 **Burgers**

 **Burritos**

**Wine Geek, Wednesday Wine**

Argentina

# Finca Las Moras

2013 Paz Malbec
$16.79

**It's fun exploring wines from up-and-coming regions.** Sure, the classic wine lands are classic for a reason. But looking off-the-beaten-vineyard path can yield some new and exciting flavour profiles. It's not Mendoza but the Pedernal Valley in San Juan Province of Argentina that's turning out some magnificent Malbec, including this bottle. Paz pours a dark, dark purple garnet and throws off intense aromas of dark fruit, plush vanilla, and pepper spice. It's quite concentrated and smooth, with sweet fruit to conclude.

Aged Parmesan

Tacos al pastor

Romance, BYO

PAZ

DE FINCA LAS MORAS

MALBEC
SAN JUAN CUYO ARGENTINA

7790240093780

Italy

# Monte del Frá

2013 Bardolino
$16.99

**New vintage, same great taste.**
Which is why Monte del Frá's
spritely red is back this year.
Now spritely isn't an adjective I
use too often to describe red
wine, but in this case it's apt.
This bodacious Bardolino has
an easygoing, super-fresh, fun-
to-quaff style. An invigorating
mix of Corvina, Rondinella,
and Sangiovese grapes (classic
red grapes used in the
Bardolino region of northeast-
ern Italy) harvested from
55-year-old vines, the wine
showcases a bright ruby colour
and tart raspberry fruit and
pairs up well with pizza—or
anything tomato sauce–based.

 Mozzarella di bufala

Pepperoni and sausage
pizza

Wine Geek, Patio/Picnic

838547000180

Chile

# Viña Tabalí

**2013 Reserva Pinot Noir**
**$17.29**

**Talk about a punchy Pinot Noir!** Redolent with fresh berry fruit and juiciness but defined by ample acidity, this spritely bottle from Viña Tabalí is both a fun solo sipper and a seriously food-friendly red. Credit is due to the Limarí Valley, a region in northern Chile that basks its vineyards in a cooling coastal influence, a geographic benefit to nicely offset the area's intense pre-desert sun. It goes gangbusters with char siu pork, not to mention mushroom duxelles.

 Roast char siu style

Mushroom duxelles pastry puff

Wine Geek, Wednesday Wine

British Columbia

# Tinhorn Creek

2012 Merlot
$17.39

**Me and Tinhorn Creek go way back.** At least way back as far as B.C. wine and my career go, which is circa 2000 (admittedly, Tinhorn Creek has been going strong in the South Okanagan since 1993). And while I've always appreciated the quality of Tinhorn's bottle lineup, I have sometimes felt overwhelmed by the "bigness" of their red wines. But the latest vintage of Merlot took me back, made me feel safe and cozy with its mix of dark fruit, toasty oak, and savoury bramble. Sure, it's plush, but there's structure too, with rich fruit leading to a grippy, cedar-imbued finish. It's not easy getting good balance in a wine this bold, and the tasty effort is certainly appreciated.

 Turkey pot pie

Chili

Classic, Winter Warmer

Italy

# Calatroni

**2012 Bonarda**
**$17.49**

**Here's a bottle with oomph and pizzazz without the pomp and circumstance.** Too many wines try too hard to impress. Calatroni's Bonarda does not. That said, as a result of its lay-it-all-out-there juiciness—not to mention punchy berry fruit and lifted floral aromatics—this gregarious red can't help but win over the taste buds. Made from 100% Croatina grapes grown in the Oltrepò Pavese region of northwestern Italy, it's plush, fresh, and balanced, a killer trifecta for the dining table.

BONARDA

Calatroni

8034055990032

 Smoked chicken

Stewed tongue

 Wine Geek, Winter Warmer

# Famiglia Bianchi

**2012 Reserva Malbec**
**$17.49**

**Go big or go for another bottle!**
If you're looking for light or crisp, stay away from this Malbec. But if you're looking for brooding, bold, and polished, then by all means continue. After 12 months in French oak barrels, this Malbec is unabashedly plush, with supple dark fruit, bitter dark chocolate, and lots of wood spice. It's even a bold, deep violet colour. Yet for all its concentration and power (more of that wood spice), it's tied together nicely, with good balance and an elegant finish.

On its own

Prime rib

Rock Out, BYO

899911000069

British Columbia

# Mission Hill

**2013 Five Vineyards Pinot Noir**
**$17.49**

**As you might suppose, the grapes used to make this wine come from five estate vineyards throughout the Okanagan.** So while 100% Pinot Noir, the fruit is a blend of different microclimates and soils. Actually, this year's Five Vineyards Pinot Noir is sourced from four vineyards: Black Sage Bench (68%), Mission Hill Road (15%), Osoyoos (12%), and Naramata Ranch (5%). After nine months in French and American oak, this mélange manifests in aromas of berry and forest floor, followed by a juicy entry with a lick of spice. Pretty classic B.C. Pinot, it's fruit-forward but not heavy and finishes fresh.

 On its own

 Grilled salmon

 Romance, Winter Warmer

Italy

# Verso

2013 Rosso Salento
$17.49

**Holy concentration!** This is
what big, fulsome wine is all
about. The stage is set with a
bold, dark colour, and from
there it's just full-on rich, plush
flavours. Dark fruit and raisin
abound (reminiscent of an appassimento, or partially dried,
style) in this sumptuous blend
of Negroamaro, Primitivo, and
Malvasia Nera from southern
Italy. Serve up with equally bold
and rich comfort dishes or a big
hunk of hard cheese.

 Aged pecorino

 Braised cheeks

 Wednesday Wine, Winter
Warmer

8008863039023

Chile

# Falernia

**2012 Reserva Carménère**
**$17.99**

**Appassimento heads to Chile, and the result is a sumptuous kiss for the taste buds.** The appassimento style, or using semi-dried grapes to make wine, has been popularized by northern Italian wineries but is used around the world. Falernia, a winery in Chile's northern Elqui Valley, partially dries their high-altitude-grown Carménère grapes on the vine. The result in the glass is super rich and concentrated but surprisingly approachable and balanced, with a panoply of sweet dark fruit and savoury cedar.

On its own

Prime rib roast

Wine Geek, Romance

7809623200322

Italy

# Fontanafredda

2013 Briccotondo Barbera
$17.99

**Here's your entry ticket into the wonderful world of northern Italian red wines.** In these parts, Nebbiolo and Barbera reign supreme (though Dolcetto is also worth a taste), and while it's unlikely you'll find a Nebbiolo in the Had a Glass price range, here we have a great example of Barbera at a tantalizing price. The Briccotondo is 100% Barbera, aged in small- and medium-sized French oak barrels, which shows dark fruit and toasty wood notes, with great intensity and a vibrant, dry finish.

 Crescenza

Stroganoff

Classic, Winter Warmer

8000174004127

Portugal

# Pedra Cancela

**2010 Dão Seleçáo de Eńologo**
**$17.99**

**Quite rich yet remarkably fresh.** This is high praise for a wine, as in a way it's akin to killing two birds with one stone—or one wine, as it were. It's not easy to showcase bold and rich dark fruit alongside elegance and lip-smacking traits, but this bottle of Pedra Cancela does so with aplomb, adding engaging herbs and nicely integrated oak as well. And while the name may read fancy, it just means that this blend of Touriga-Nacional, Alfrocheiro, and Tinta Roriz is the "Winemaker's Selection," which is always a wise choice!

Grilled tri-tip

Grilled chops

 Wine Geek, Winter Warmer

5600376952009

Australia

# Longview

2013 Shiraz Cabernet Sauvignon
$18.29

**This is a red blend made for the barbeque.** Lifted aromas of berry fruit, eucalypt, and vanilla lead to a super-ripe, fruity entry. But right when you think things are headed over the top, the Longview Shiraz Cab holds back mid-palate, allowing toasty oak and peppery spice to build before a woodsy, dry finish. The total wine experience is thus full on but approachable, a bod number ready to tackle high BTUs.

Spicy sticky ribs

Prime rib

BYO, Patio/Picnic

Argentina

# La Posta

**2013 Pizzella Malbec**
**$18.99**

**Good wine is all about flavour.**
And great wine is all about
layers of flavour. La Posta's
Pizzella Malbec is of the darker
colour, deeper flavour, and
downright more brooding disposition. Scents of smoked
meat, fruit, and toasty oak whiff
out of the glass in this rich
Malbec, which is robust yet polished, with complex layers of
flavour and ample character—
all wrapped up in that cool,
classy font-heavy label.

Grilled rib eye

Grilled chops

Rock Out, Classic

835603001310

# Maison des Bulliats

2013 Régnié
$19.29

**Well, it's happened.** Last year I was concerned that the rising popularity of Beaujolais was pushing prices beyond the Had a Glass fencepost. And indeed many of the Cru Beaujolais and even Beaujolais-Villages have priced themselves out of contention. But Maison des Bulliats is barely hanging on, and considering that it's such a delicious and important style of wine it makes another run. It's still the best Cru for the money, still full of the tasty essence of the Gamay grape (that beguiling combination of fruit and bramble, perfume and earth), and still wonderfully intense for such a light and vibrant red wine.

On its own

Barbequed tri-tip

Wine Geek, Romance

France

# Famille Perrin

### 2011 L'Andéol Rasteau
### $19.49

**Less oak, more filling!** Too much oak in a wine is akin to hydrogenated vegetable oil. Sure, the influence of toasty oak can certainly add to a wine, but it must complement, not dominate—let the grapes' true character and flavour fill the wine. For Famille Perrin's Rasteau, only 10% of the grapes see time in oak, and they're large oak Foudres at that. As a result, the voluptuous Grenache and peppery Syrah star, the wine is bold and gutsy without any filler.

 Duck breast

Comté

 Winter Warmer, Rock Out

Spain

# Vivanco

2010 Rioja Crianza
$19.59

**Rioja is the patriarch of Spanish wine regions, the Grand Pooh-Bah of the country's vinous affairs.** Indeed, grapes have been grown and wine has been made in this part of Spain for more than 1,000 years, and its produce still resonates today in a myriad of incarnations helpfully labelled Crianza, Reserva, and Gran Reserva. The Crianza tag dictates at least one year of oak aging and one year in bottle, as is the case with Vivanco's peppy Rioja. Pouring a bright garnet, this Miro-labelled bottle offers classic Rioja aromas of black cherry and toasty oak before settling into a more modern, fruity yet fresh style with balance and finesse to finish.

 Mushroom tart

Shepherd's pie

Winter Warmer, BYO

South Africa

# Glen Carlou

**2011 Grand Classique**
**$19.99**

**Sometimes I find myself in the mood for a lush yet dignified red.** In these moments, I can count on Glen Carlou's Grand Classique. It's a perennial go-to bottle that consistently delivers dense, complex layers of flavour without sacrificing sang-froid. This mix of Cabernet Sauvignon, Malbec, Merlot, Petit Verdot, and Cabernet Franc (the five classic grape varieties in Red Bordeaux) from Paarl sees 18 months aging in new- and second-fill oak barrels, and the end result is a winning combination of robust ripe fruit and integrated toasty wood notes that manages to be both in-your-face and graceful.

 On its own

 Sauerbraten

Winter Warmer,
Romance

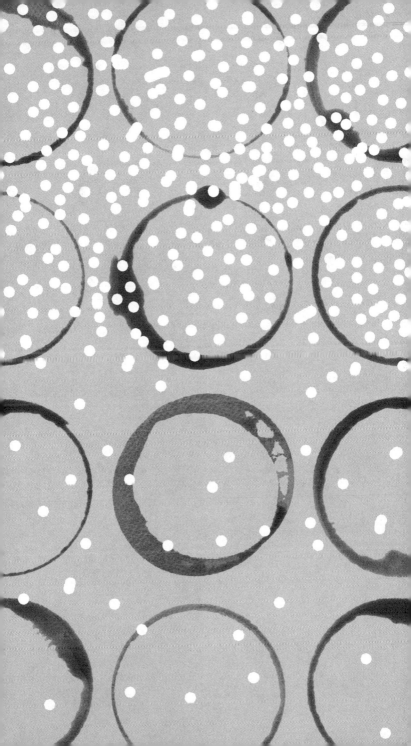

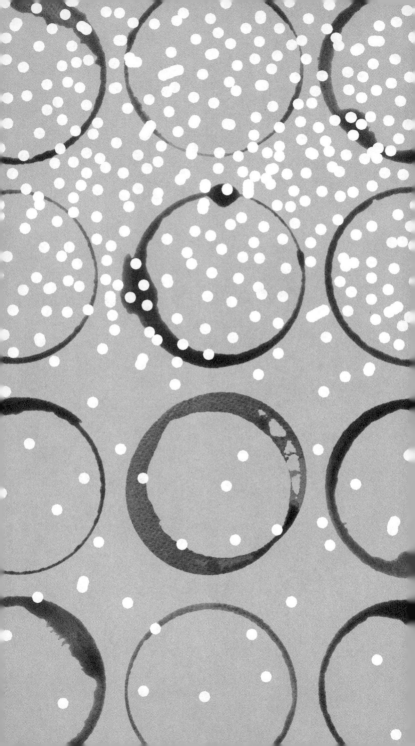

# The Sparkling

Spain

# Jaume Serra

**Cristalino Brut Cava**
**$11.29**

**I am not going to apologize for having this Brut Cava appear in Had a Glass year in and year out.** Think that Woody Allen feels sorry for wearing thick-rimmed black plastic glasses year after year? This is sparkling wine for 364 days of the year, for those days that don't require something fancy-schmancy, for those times when sparkling wine cocktails are in order or you simply want a palate cleanser to sip in between mouthfuls of bacon and eggs Benny.

On its own

Hash brown

Wednesday Wine, Classic

France

# Marquis de la Tour

**Brut**
**$13.29**

**Sparkling wine shouldn't be stashed solely to celebrate a birthday or a new year.** Pop a cork when you get a good deal on a pair of shoes or when your fantasy football team makes the cut. The Marquis is the perfect everyday bubbly; it's dry and fresh, with pleasing apple aromas and a hint of the bubbly's trademark toastiness. Have a flute neat or mix with OJ for the weekend brunch. Solid value.

 **On its own**

 **Bacon and eggs**

 **Wednesday Wine, Patio/ Picnic**

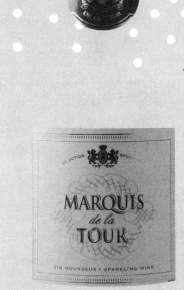

3221580029435

Spain

# Segura Viudas

**Brut Rosado Cava**
**$14.79**

**Sparkling rosé is the most versatile style of wine there is.** Period. It's food-friendly—balancing the freshness of a crisp white wine with the richness of a red—and adds the tickle of bubbles for good measure. Plus, while it's not like celebration is mandatory for breaking out the fizz, the fact that it can pull celebratory double-duty further elevates its all-round appeal. For a tasty version that won't break the bank, Segura Viudas's exuberant Rosado delivers, featuring candied cherry fruit, a robust overall stance, and a balanced, easygoing but dry finish.

Brie and cranberry jelly

Country terrine

 BYO, Wednesday Wine

33293640004

# Villa Conchi

**Brut Selección Cava**
**$15.79**

**A classy label and a classy Cava.** One could do much worse than bring this bottle to a friend's open house. Sporting a 10% dollop of Chardonnay to the typical Cava triumvirate of Macabeo, Xarel-lo, and Parellada, Villa Conchi spews great aromas of lemon, herbs, and earth. It's sharper and drier than many of the other sparklers on these pages, yet this Cava manages nice richness and depth before its bone-dry finish. Serve up with a meal's worth of tapas for a fun evening.

**Patatas bravas**

**Gambas al Ajillo**

**Rock Out, BYO**

8437012435285

Italy

# Bottega

**Il Vino dei Poeti Prosecco**
**$17.29**

**This is feisty bubbly.** Popping the cork unveils an aggressive mousse, which actually turns into more of a tickle on the tongue. Along the way, great classic aromas of citrus and peach abound, and a fulsome body coats the mouth. Slightly off-dry but nice and crisp on a robust finish, add a piazza with this stylish Prosecco and you've got good times.

On its own

Cream cheese on crackers

Patio/Picnic, BYO

8005829221317

Spain

# Parés Baltà

**Brut Cava**
**$18.49**

Organically
Grown

**This Brut Cava pours a delightful straw colour with subtle green tinges.** Pear and apple aromas waft from this spritely Spanish sparkler, which is made from the three classic Cava grapes (Parellada, Macabeo, and Xarel-lo) that are organically grown in the Penedès region near Barcelona. Fantastically fresh and crisply acidic, this lighter-bodied sparkling wine is perfect paired with crab cakes or fried chicken, or simply an inviting seat on a patio.

 On its own

Crab cakes

 Patio/Picnic, BYO

8410439034354

British Columbia

# See Ya Later Ranch

**SYL Brut**
**$19.99**

**Over the years See Ya Later Ranch's SYL Brut has proven a solid go-to sparkler.** Produced using the Traditional Method, this quirky blend of Chardonnay and Riesling sits for three years *en tirage*, or in contact with the lees, before disgorging and bottling. The result in the glass is fresh and fruity, featuring aromas of Panetonne, lemon zest, and orchard fruit. After a juicy approach it comes across quite dry and crisp; this breezy Brut goes great with brunch or seafood.

 Watermelon and feta salad

 Smoked salmon on bagels

 Wednesday Wine, Rock Out

624738011048

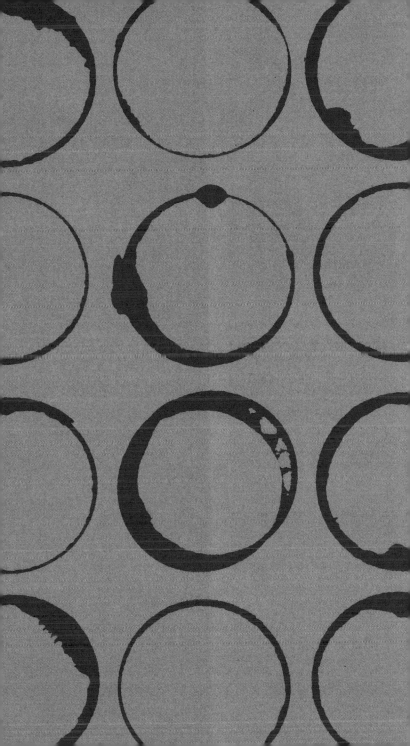

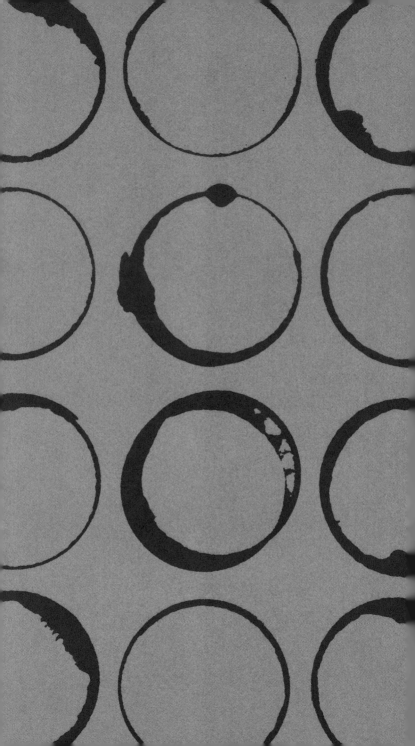

# The Fortifieds

Portugal

# Warre's

**Warrior Reserve Port**
**$11.79 for 375 mL**

**Unfortunately, there's a dearth of value-priced ports available locally.** Fortunately, Warre's Warrior Reserve Port remains on the shelves and is one fantastic option. So it's back in *Had a Glass* to fulfill an important role in every wine fan's repertoire. For wine doesn't just end at the whites and reds (or perhaps the pinks and sparkling). No, it's important to flip to the end of the book (or the end of the meal, as it were) and remember the fortified wines! Despite its combative name, this port is actually rather easygoing, full of rich dark fruit, some baking spices, and a sumptuous mouthfeel that makes a fine tipple to end the evening.

On its own

Stilton

Classic, Romance

British Columbia

# Gehringer Brothers

**2014 Late Harvest Riesling**
**$15.69 for 375mL**

**Sure, ice wine has all the status.** But for my money, I'll take late-harvest wine as my de facto decadent wine pick. Picking grapes at subzero temperatures frames a romantic notion (as long as you're not the one freezing your fingers!), but simply allowing grapes to linger on the vines well past typical harvest date also creates great flavour concentration. The end result is a sumptuous mélange of ripe stone fruit and baked apple, rich and honeyed, yet with ample acidity to keep the finish fresh. It's great sipped on its own or paired with a hunk of cheese for dessert (the saltier the better).

Peanut brittle

Cambazolo

Winter Warmer, BYO

United States

# Quady

**Essensia Orange Muscat**
**$15.79 for 375mL**

**Here's a delectable dessert wine/perfect nightcap.**
California's Quady only crafts sweet and aperitif wines, which is not the easiest path for a winery to follow. Admittedly, too many wine enthusiasts overlook the sweet stuff and fortifieds. But one taste of the Essensia Orange Muscat will show how sweet wines provide a unique, and important, perspective on overall wine enjoyment. Great candied orange peel aromatics lead to a sumptuous, plump, and orangey midpalate. Sure, it's sweet as expected, but acidity bridges a balance to finish.

On its own

Dark chocolate

Romance, Wine Geek

# Lillet

Blanc
$16.49

**Lillet continues its Had a Glass run.** For good reason. It is a versatile, verifiable classic bottle steeped in aperitif-ian history. Of course, this aromatic fortified wine from France also happens to be steeped in a secret blend of macerated liqueurs created mostly from a bevy of citrus peels, which is the key to Lillet's lip-smacking prowess. Melding a balance of bitter and sweet, it is perfect for solo sipping with a slice of orange or lemon during the approach to dinner but also deftly adds a layer of flavour in famous cocktails such as the Vesper and Corpse Reviver #2. And remember, with only an ounce used here and there, a bottle of Lillet tends to go a long way.

On its own

Salted nuts

Classic, Patio/Picnic

Spain

# Lustau

**Puerto Fino Sherry**
**$16.59 for 375 mL**

**Sipping this is like having a bolt of lightning hit your tongue.** Fino sherries are known for their bracing dryness, and to drive home the point Lustau helpfully splashes Muy seco, or "very dry," across the front label. Indeed, there's an invigorating tanginess, a brininess, an austerity even, that not only puckers the lips but makes one sit up and notice. And in this moment you realize there's more: layers of complexity and savoury tones, dimensions that make this one fine sipping sherry, not just on its own but as a partner for any deep-fried foods.

Pan-toasted almonds

Calamari

 Wednesday Wine, Classic

Italy

# Florio

2011 Vecchioflorio Marsala
Superiore Dolce
$16.89

**Sure, Marsala is great for cooking, but it makes for fine sipping too.** It's time to switch up your fortified wine routine! Like port, this storied fortified from the Italian isle of Sicily has varying designations, with Marsala Superiore indicating that the wine is aged at least two years. A gorgeous amber colour, it's rich and ripe and oozes raisin and dates, vanilla and caramel. It's a fine after-dinner treat that seriously warms the cockles, and small pours mean the bottle will have some staying power (just don't forget about it in the fridge door!).

 Crackers and cream cheese

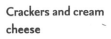 Butter tarts

Wine Geek, Romance

891006001012

Spain

# Alvear

**Medium Dry**
**$17.29**

**Here's a sweet wine for non-fans of sweet wine.** Seriously. While this Spanish fortified certainly comes across rich and sweet, it is anything but cloying. This is a great introduction to the unique amontillado style, which is essentially a fino sherry minus its protective cap of flor, which undergoes a slow, flavour-enhancing oxidation. It pours a rich bronze in the glass, and on first sip it coats the mouth with savoury, classic nutty and dried-fruit flavours. The finish is bold but deft, with no syrupy heaviness, making this an amenable fortified. Serve cold from the fridge.

On its own

Cabrales

Rock Out, Classic

SPECIAL
**10**TH
ANNIVERSARY
EDITION

# Guest Wine Reviews

# Kurtis Kolt

Kurtis Kolt is the weekly wine columnist for The Georgia Straight, a seriously multitasking independent wine consultant, and all-around cool guy. I've had the pleasure of sharing many wine experiences with Kurtis, not to mention that we share the same birthday—how cool is that!

 **Your top under–$20 wine pick?**
**Gonzalez Byass Nutty Solera Oloroso, Spain ($15.69)**

"I like to think of the Nutty Solera as a 'gateway sherry,' as it's an easy-to-like introduction to such a charming category of wine. Served with a bit of a chill, its flavours of roasted hazelnuts, cashews and almonds—along with a smidge of toffee—make it a worthy companion to strong cheeses, cured meats, wild mushroom risotto, and so much more."

8410023020138

# John Schreiner

John Schreiner is the B.C. wine authority. He's been following the local wine scene for decades, he's written more books on B.C. wine than anyone, and the information contained within is always illuminating and informative. Plus, as I've been fortunate to learn on occasions when we have shared stages and judging tables, he's amazingly generous in sharing his wisdom.

 **Your top under–$20 wine pick?**
**Arrowleaf Cellars 2014 First Crush Rosé, British Columbia ($13.49)**

"Arrowleaf Cellars is a family-owned winery in Lake Country that offers reasonably priced wines in its entire portfolio. This rosé is especially good value. A blend of Pinot Noir and Zweigelt, it is made with grapes harvested a week or two before the varieties are picked for red wine. This ensures moderate alcohol and refreshing acidity. The crushed grapes are soaked on the skins long enough to produce a vibrant salmon pink hue. The Pinot Noir delivers aromas and flavours of strawberry, while the Zweigelt adds cherry and cranberry. The dry finish makes this a versatile food wine."

626990155171

# Treve Ring

Treve Ring has to be one of the nicest, most generous wine pros I know. But don't let the niceties fool you, as she also has one of the meanest, baddest palates around. It's hard to pin her down; she always seems to be on the go, tasting and touring the wine world in order to share the wine love with her audiences at Wine Align and www.gismondionwine.com, to name but a few!

 **Your top under–$20 wine pick?**
**Pagos Familia Langa Real de Aragon Cava, Spain ($13.29)**

"We should all drink more bubble, and with this stellar organic sparkling wine at this price, there is no excuse not to celebrate. Bonus—the pretty label will brighten your brunch table or canapés affair. From the highlands of Calatayud, this crisp sparkler charms from the first nutty, green–apple whiff to the tart quince and lemon palate, through the persistent white grapefruit pith and sea salt finish. Bright and friendly but serious Cava."

626990121626

# Rhys Pender, MW

I met Rhys Pender while I was working in a Vancouver wine shop. It was the best retail job I ever had, not to mention that it's where I cut my teeth on wine (not literally, of course). Now Rhys, MW (he's an acclaimed Master of Wine!), travels the wine world tasting, judging, teaching, writing, and consulting on wine. And when he's at home, he helps run Little Farm Winery, the four-acre (1.6-hectare) Similkameen Valley winery he co-owns with his equally cool partner, Alishan Driediger.

**Your top under–$20 wine pick?**
**Yering Station 2013 Little Yering Pinot Noir, Australia ($14.49)**

"Pinot Noir that is both delicious and inexpensive is too rare. Pinot also isn't the first grape we associate with Australia. But this wine is Australian, delicious, and a bargain. It has plenty of varietal character with lots of red berry fruit but also some of those savoury, earthy, meaty notes that make it serious Pinot. Dry, savoury, juicy, and tasty . . . what more do you need?"

659284000581

# Michelle Bouffard

Michelle Bouffard was another co-conspirator at that little Vancouver wine store back in the day, where we shared tastes and swapped wine tales from morning to night (or at least until 9:00 p.m. when the store closed and we had to cash out!). Today, Michelle teaches the Wine and Spirit Education Trust's (WSET) program across Canada (she holds an International Sommelier Diploma and WSET Diploma). For the past 12 years she has co-owned Vancouver-based House Wine, along the way completing tons of consulting, writing, media, and judging projects.

 **Your top under–$20 wine pick?**
**Ormarine Picpoul de Pinet, France ($14.79)**

"From year to year, this bottle never disappoints. The Southern French white grape Picpoul produces a wine with bright and thirst-quenching notes of lemon and mineral. A passe-partout for all occasions, you will enjoy Ormarine as much with seafood pasta, oysters, asparagus salad, or ceviche as you will on its own as an aperitif. And there is nothing better to accompany your game of pétanque. It will improve your game greatly; trust me. Santé!"

3186127768690

# Michaela Morris

Michaela Morris is the other co-owner of House Wine, and she's the weekly wine columnist for the *Westender* newspaper and a contributor to other august publications including EAT and TASTE magazines. Of course, it goes without saying that her experienced palate is in high demand at judgings and tastings around the world, and she was recently certified as an Italian Wine Ambassador through the Vinitaly International Academy!

 **Your top under–$20 wine pick?**
**Rilento 2012 Nerello Mascalese, Italy**
**($12.79)**

"With hundreds of indigenous grape varieties, Italy is a treasure trove for the wine adventurous. One of these gems is Nerello Mascalese from Sicily. Appetizing aromas of balsam, tea, and sun-dried herb are followed by a mouthful of exotic herb flowers and wild cherries. The juicy acid, subtle tannic grip, and savouriness make me hungry. What more could you ask for from a wine? Just add a plate of Italian fennel sausage for maximum enjoyment."

8033765259392

# Tim Pawsey

Over the years, Tim and I have shared some great wine times, whether cruising the back roads of the Okanagan Valley or the downtown streets of Paso Robles. You likely know Tim as "The Hired Belly" from his posts on www.hiredbelly.com or from his work in a number of publications, including the North Shore News, WHERE, Quench, and TASTE magazines. Wherever his words or pictures appear, a constant of Tim's that I never tire of is his upbeat, accessible take on food and wine.

 **Your top under–$20 wine pick?**
**Tahbilk 2013 Marsanne, Australia ($17.79)**

"Ultimately, it's all about not just bargain wines but value-priced wines that are interesting and maybe even overdeliver. I like wines that make a point of difference. One of the best (still unsung) values ever (which I've been buying for 20-plus years) is Chateau Tahbilk Marsanne. Forget about Chardonnay and have a crack at this really impressive long-running, old-vines Aussie white instead—which actually might remind you more of Viognier. Packed with citrus, honey, and stone fruit—you'll even find a splash of mineral—wrapped up in juicy acidity. Pair it with scallops, acorn squash, or cracked Dungeness crab and lemon butter."

93121631000793

# Sebastien Le Goff

Sebastien Le Goff is one of the most charismatic wine guys I know. That accent, that wine prowess, the man is simply a machine around the tasting table—it's darn near impossible to keep up. Not surprisingly, this has led to accolades, including Sebastien being named Sommelier of the Year by numerous bodies, and today he is the service director for Cactus Club Cafe.

 **Your top under–$20 wine pick?**
**Quinta dos Grilos 2012 Tondela, Portugal ($13.29)**

"This red wine from the northern part of Portugal features grapes typical to port. Upon opening the bottle and pouring a first glass, the wine boasts lots of plum, spices, oregano, and leather. The wine's tannins mean business, but they are soft and allow for a great quaffing wine. The acidity is also quite refreshing. The wine gets even better the next day with lots of raspberry notes and a softer approach. Enjoy with pork or lamb chops on the barbeque, or on a picnic with cheese and cold cuts. Unbelievable quality for its price. A great everyday, drinking-value red."

5604575000417

# Sid Cross

Sid Cross is a legend in the wine world. And I'm not just talking locally. Sid is globally respected, and for good reason. I don't think I've met someone more knowledgeable about wine—with the ability to recall tasting notes from his seemingly inexhaustive mental wine database. Really, his accomplishments are too long to list, but even so, he remains amazingly down-to-earth and encouraging, always ready to share a glass while asking how everything is going.

 **Your top under–$20 wine pick?**
**Spierhead Winery 2014 Pinot Gris, British Columbia ($19.00)**

"There is a plethora of B.C. Pinot Gris out there, from boring to oniony-garlic flavoured to light pink rose colours. I heartily endorse this estate-grown effort, 710 cases produced from Golden Retreat Vineyard in Summerland that is aged 10 months in 30% new French oak and 70% stainless steel. It combines enticing aromas of tropical fruit, peaches, melon, citrus, and apples, showing creamy, full-bodied flavours with attractive mineral freshness. Delicious!"

626990212232

# Anthony Gismondi

I've been fortunate to know Anthony Gismondi for years, even if back in the day he teased me about my wine-tasting toque when I was the young 'un on the wine scene. Anthony is the long-standing wine columnist for The Vancouver Sun, a partner and principal critic for Wine Align, and the creator of www.gismondionwine.com. Essentially, he spends his time travelling the world looking for good wines and good wine tales to tell.

**Your top under–$20 wine pick?**
**Louis Bernard 2014 Côtes du Rhône Blanc, France ($13.99)**

"White Rhône may not be at the top of your white wine list, but this wine is as delicious as ever for the price and a real revelation regarding white Rhône. The blend is a mix of Grenache Blanc, Bourboulenc, and Clairette, and it is as juicy and as fresh as it comes for the price. Expect a floral, mineral, citrus, stony white wine that is very food-friendly. The finish is clean and dry. Pick your favourite seafood or creamy pasta dish, they will all work."

604174000974

SPECIAL
**10**TH
ANNIVERSARY
EDITION

# The Best of 10 Years

It truly is incredible to consider that this edition of Had a Glass marks a culmination of 10 years of wining. To momentarily lapse into cliché, it really has been about the journey more than the destination. And, as the adventure-at-hand has been tasting (and enjoying) wine, it has not been a terribly difficult path to pursue.

A decade's worth of tasting offers interesting insight into wine trends. For instance, when Had a Glass was first published, we were caught in a serious closure kerfuffle. The debate between cork versus screw cap was just underway. Nowadays, would anyone look askance at any wine bottle encased with metal?

Over the years the origin of the wines in Had a Glass has also matured, and it's interesting to compare and contrast the wines that have featured in these pages. There has been a noticeable trend toward the Old World of wine, with bottles from Italy, Spain, and France most represented. That said, there's never been more diverse geography featured, and more than 15 different-ent wine-producing nations are now highlighted in these pages. It's a trend mirrored on the shelves in wine stores, as wine buyers seek out both classic and new wines from around the world. Over the past 10 years, previously esoteric bottles have mainstreamed, while wines from even more remote and lesser-known regions have begun appearing on local shelves. Thus, wine drinkers can find more options from the Rhône Valley, just as they'll increasingly see bottles from up-and-coming regions in Chile such as Elqui and Bío-Bío; and Assyrtiko and Grüner Veltliner grapes, while still perhaps exotic, are less than alien; and cool-climate hunters can rejoice at finding wines from Australia's Limestone Coast.

Regardless of variety or provenance, *Had a Glass* wines share a foundation of good flavour and great character. For example, more unique wines have always found a home in *Had a Glass*: Quinta do Crasto's gutsy Douro red blend from Portugal made an appearance in the first edition (the 2001 vintage), and it was there again last year (2012 vintage), still at a price point of $19.99 no less! Of course, over the years evolving tastes and preferences have led to an changing selection of bottles, say, from a range of Cava and Prosecco in sparkling wine to a move for more Malbec versus Merlot. Currently, there seems to be growing consumer interest in lower-alcohol, higher-acidity wines of all types, and there's a burgeoning representation of extremely versatile rosé lining the shelves.

Oh, and then there's price. In 2006, a litre of gas cost about a buck and the average price of the wines in *Had a Glass* hovered around $14.50. Today, not so much, and it's probably not surprising to note that overall the price of wines in *Had a Glass* has crept toward that $20 upper bound. Now, it would be nice to simply blame inflation, but in reality those killer bottles rarely stay at their lower price point (particularly when the super-value word spreads), and indeed there has been a general trend to move away from bargain basement bottles.

Of course, the more things change, the more they stay the

same (whoops, there's a cliché again!), and there has always been a place for straight-up, big-value bottles in Had a Glass. Classic, $10-ish wines that don't overpromise and therefore can overdeliver will never go out of style. This is why names such as Castillo de Monséran, La Bastide, Cono Sur, Dunavar, Finca Los Primos, and Las Pergolas continue to make regular appearances in these pages. The vintages may change, but when budgets must be adhered to, year in and year out picking up one of these bottles is a vinous value no-brainer.

Throughout the years the list of Top 100 wines has been a constant, but the rest of Had a Glass has permuted to reflect whims and personal perspective. From recipes and wine pairings to wine cocktails, not to mention beyond-$20 bottle asides, Had a Glass has offered a marriage of fun and accessible living with wine. And while it's hard to pinpoint absolute favourites, the following retrospective represents a particularly personal "best of" list of favourite Had a Glass moments from the past 10 years.

# Easy Pasta Puttanesca

A dear family friend, Mimi, provided significant inspiration for getting into the good life. The early years of Had a Glass featured a number of Mimi-approved, easy-to-prepare and easy-to-pair meals. This pasta dish, a classic from the 2006 edition, remains an everyday favourite.

Prep: 15 minutes  |  Cook: 15 minutes  |  Makes: 4 servings
Wine pairing: Castiglioni Chianti (page 119)

| | |
|---|---|
| 4 tbsp (50 mL) | olive oil |
| ½ cup (125 mL) | onions, chopped |
| 2 tbsp (30 mL) | capers, chopped |
| ¼ cup (50 mL) | Kalamata olives, sliced |
| 2 tbsp (30 mL) | garlic, chopped |
| 4 tsp (20 mL) | anchovies, chopped |
| 2 cups (500 mL) | cherry tomatoes, halved |
| large handful | fresh basil, chopped |
| ¼ cup (50 mL) | fresh Italian parsley, chopped |
| a pinch | chili flakes |
| generous pinch | salt |
| 12 oz (350 g) | dried pasta |
| to taste | freshly grated Parmesan cheese |

Heat heavy-bottomed saucepan over medium heat. Add olive oil and pinch of salt. Add onions and cook until softened but not brown. Add capers, olives, garlic, and anchovies and simmer for 1 minute. Add cherry tomatoes, basil, parsley, and chili flakes and simmer for 5 minutes.

Cook pasta according to package directions. Drain pasta, reserving ½ cup (125 mL) pasta water. Toss pasta, water, and sauce together. Top with freshly grated Parmesan just before serving.

# Machaca Beef Burritos

This is how my mom made machaca beef while I was growing up. It first appeared in Had a Glass 2007 and it's the recipe I still use to this day. We're talking gut-satisfying comfort food and a meal that goes gangbusters with smooth, rich reds and racy rosés.

**Prep: 15 minutes** | **Cook: about 3 hours** | **Makes: 8 servings**
**Wine pairing:** Painted Wolf The Den Pinotage (page 118)

| | |
|---|---|
| 2 tbsp (30 mL) | canola oil |
| to taste | salt and pepper |
| 2–3 lb (1.5 kg) | beef chuck roast |
| 1 | large onion, chopped |
| 1 | green pepper, chopped |
| 2 | cloves garlic, minced |
| ½ | jalapeño pepper, minced |
| 2 | 14-oz (398 mL) cans, diced tomatoes |
| 1–2 tsp (5–10 mL) | dried oregano |
| ½–1 tsp (2.5–5 mL) | ground cumin |
| 12 | flour tortillas |

In a large, heavy-bottomed stock pot, heat oil over medium-high heat. Salt and pepper beef roast and sear a few minutes on each side until brown. Remove from pot.

Add onions, peppers, and garlic and sauté until soft. Add the remaining ingredients to the pot, including beef, and bring to a boil (trying to scrape the good, tasty brown bits from the bottom of the pot). Reduce heat, cover, and simmer until the beef is very tender (about 3 hours). Machaca is ready when it pulls apart with forks. Using two forks, completely shred beef. If there's too much liquid, increase heat and reduce until sauce is thickened.

Warm tortillas, fill with machaca beef and any other toppings, wrap, and enjoy.

# 🐔 Coq au Vin

In the 2008 edition of Had a Glass, the recipes were all about wine-savviness—specifically recipes that called for cooking with wine. This included the classic, and consistently foolproof, favourite French one-pot wonder. But in a twist, the Had a Glass rendition calls for both red and white wine.

**Prep:** 30 minutes | **Cook:** about 1.5 hours | **Makes:** 4 servings
**Wine pairing:** DeMorgenzon DMZ Chardonnay (page 83)

| | |
|---|---|
| 1 | large chicken, or 8 thighs |
| 4 slices | bacon, cut into ½-in. (1 cm) strips |
| 1 tbsp (15 mL) | butter |
| 2 | medium onions, chopped |
| 2 | carrots, coarsely chopped |
| 2 | celery sticks, chopped |
| 2 tbsp (30 mL) | flour |
| ½ bottle (375 mL) | red wine (avoid heavy oaked red) |
| ½ bottle (375 mL) | white wine |
| 4–5 sprigs | fresh thyme (or 1 tsp/5 mL dried) |
| 2 | bay leaves |
| 12 | pearl onions |
| 10–12 | white mushrooms, halved |

In a heavy-bottomed pot, melt the butter on medium heat and fry the bacon until it looks like Saturday morning's breakfast. Remove to a large bowl. In the same pot, add the chicken parts— skin side down—into the greasy goodness. When the chicken has turned pale golden, turn over and repeat for opposite side. When completely golden, remove to the bacon bowl. In the even greasier goodness, add the onions, carrots, and celery. Sauté the veggies, scraping up the sticky bits left over from the chicken. When the onions are translucent, add the mushrooms and sauté for another couple of minutes.

Now place the chicken and bacon back into the pot, add the flour, and mix to coat. Add the wine, thyme, bay leaves, and enough stock or water to cover the chicken. Bring to a boil, then quickly turn down to a simmer, and cook covered for about 45 minutes.

Check the chicken. The meat should be separating from the bone. If so, remove the chicken to plates and keep warm.

Turn up the heat on the broth and let it reduce (no cover) until it starts to thicken. Pour the reduced liquid and the veggies over the chicken, and serve with roast potatoes or steamed rice.

# Ceviche by Steve

In the 2010 Had a Glass, the recipes were solicited from a few best-cooking friends, and the collection included this super-easy and supremely tasty, not to mention sparkling-wine-superstar-partnering, fresh fish dish.

Prep: **15 minutes** | Cook: **3 hours** | Makes: **4 servings**
Wine pairing: **Villa Conchi Brut Selección Cava (page 147)**

| | |
|---|---|
| ¾ lb | fresh white fish (snapper, cod, halibut) |
| a handful | bay scallops |
| 1 | hot pepper (serrano, habañero, etc.) |
| ½ | red onion, sliced |
| 1 | clove garlic, minced |
| ⅓ cup (80 mL) | lime juice |
| 3 tbsp (45 mL) | pineapple juice |
| a splash | orange juice |
| 1 tbsp (15 mL) | olive oil |
| a handful | cilantro, chopped |
| a pinch | salt |

Cut the fish into ¼-in. (6 mm) cubes and place in a glass dish along with the scallops. Remove the seeds from the pepper, unless you love the heat, and slice thinly. Toss the pepper slices, onion, and garlic with the fish.

Next, pour the lime, pineapple, and orange juices over the mixture. Lightly toss the ingredients together to coat. Cover and place in the refrigerator for 2–3 hours. (The fish will begin to turn opaque as it marinades.)

Before serving, lightly fold in the olive oil, cilantro, and salt. Serve ceviche on top of a leaf of butter lettuce, accompanied by oven-roasted yam rounds and corn on the cob, or in a martini glass with tortilla chips.

# The Cascadian 86

The past few years of Had a Glass saw a switch to recipes for wine cocktails, including this favourite locavore sparkling number from the 2014 edition. Yes, really it's just a riff on the French 75 but with a Pacific Northwest accent.

Makes 1 cocktail

| 1 oz | Victoria gin (or as local a gin as possible)* |
| ½ oz | simple syrup |
| ½ oz | lemon juice |
| 5 oz | Brut sparkling wine (try See Ya Later Ranch SYL Brut, page 150) |

Combine gin, simple syrup, and lemon juice in a chilled cocktail shaker filled with ice and shake well. Strain into a Collins glass filled with cracked ice and top up with chilled Brut. Garnish with a twist of lemon or a sprig of Douglas fir if you're feeling really patriotic.

---

\* The original recipe calls for 2 oz gin, imbuing the drink with so much firepower that it was named after the potent French 75mm artillery gun used during the First World War. Most modern renditions, however, scale the dry gin quotient in half.

# Sherry Cobbler

Last year's edition included a collection of classic wine-based cocktails, including this easy-to-prepare Sherry Cobbler. Why it hasn't taken off to super-trend status is truly a mystery. The Sherry Cobbler is a quintessential American classic, so old school that it's cool again.

Makes 1 cocktail

| | |
|---|---|
| 4 oz | fino or amontillado sherry (try Lustau Puerto Fino Sherry, page 158) |
| 1½ tsp | superfine sugar |
| 1 | orange slice |
| 3–4 berries | (though any fruit on hand will suffice) |
| 1 | straw (the Sherry Cobbler is reputed to have popularized the straw) |

Cut the orange slice in half and stuff into a mixing glass or cocktail shaker. Fill with ice, pour in sherry, add sugar, and proceed to shake vigorously while reciting your ABCs (or at least until the sugar is dissolved). Pour into a tall Collins glass filled with fresh crushed ice, and garnish with seasonal berries. For maximum refreshment (and ease), drink through a straw.

# The Splurge

Had a Glass champions the idea that there is a wine for every occasion and every budget, but occasionally it's necessary to blow the budget! The plain truth is that certain types of wine will never fall into the under-$20 category. It doesn't mean that they're not good value, just that they're pricey for a reason. Here are the 10 splurges from Had a Glass 2013, all of which remain worthwhile budget busters.

Splurge #1:    Plus-sized bottles

Splurge #2:    Champagne

Splurge #3:    Vintage port

Splurge #4:    Or for that matter, a bottle of any good ol' sticky, fortified wine

Splurge #5:    Go au naturel! So-called "natural wines," made with minimal intervention (i.e., using organically farmed grapes, native yeasts and no chemical synthetic additives), are gaining a following.

Splurge #6:    Top-tier Riesling

Splurge #7:    Gran Reserva Rioja

Splurge #8:    Grand Cru Burgundy

Splurge #9:    A bottle from your birth year

Splurge #10:    A coffee-table-worthy wine reference book

SPECIAL
**10**TH
ANNIVERSARY
EDITION

# Top 10 Wines from
# the Last 10 Years

"What's your favourite wine?" Or, put another way, "What's the best wine you have ever tasted?" Without a doubt, over the years this is the question I have most often been asked. To be honest, it's a question I don't like answering because, well, I honestly don't have a concrete response. I'm not going to say it's like a parent being asked to choose a favourite offspring. But it is complicated. Mood, food, company, season, bottle age . . . so many factors contribute to a wine's enjoyment, and as a result "best" becomes quite relative.

Some of the cheapest bottles of wine I have sipped have been my favourites simply because of time, place, and space of consumption (I'm looking at you, *vino tinto* purchased for a few Euros in a recycled 1.5L Fanta bottle in Barcelona!). And some of the most expensive wines I have swigged have also been my favourites (I'm thinking of you, bottle of Grange served at Penfolds Magill Estate Restaurant just outside Adelaide!).

That said, looking back I can certainly say that there are wines I seem to be drawn towards. These are wines I constantly return to, that my hands instinctually reach for on the shelves (or reached for, in the case of bottles no longer available in our local market!). This is not to say that they are the "best" wines ever; indeed, a number of them are not even what I would call overly complex. I suppose the secret to their success is that they just pair well with my lifestyle in general, which really is great praise for wine.

Here, then, is my "Top 10" pick of wines that have appeared in the pages of Had a Glass over the last 10 years. Some have sadly come and gone, victims of fickle marketplace supply and demand; others may no longer fit under the imposed $20 threshold. Regardless, they are my favourites and hold special places in my mental cellar. Of course, there is no official numerical ranking for this "Top 10," because, well, mood, food, company, etc.

### Bodegas Piqueras Marques de Rojas, Spain
No oak, no fuss. Kitschy cool label, yes. For years this wine was in serious rotation as one of my everyday reds; it pushed out more flavour for 10 bucks—not to mention it was well balanced and food friendly—than most wines I have tasted.
**Wine Status: No longer available**

### Cono Sur Viognier, Chile
The definition of cheap and cheerful, without any tongue-in-cheek negative connotation. I've lost track of how many times I've recommended this exuberant white when asked for a versatile wine that won't break the bank!
**Wine Status: Still widely available, $9.79**

### Marqués de Cáceres Rosado, Spain
Years before rosé was a "thing," before there were weird articles being penned about men not having to blush while drinking

pink wine, there was Marqués de Cáceres Rosado. It was an awesome all-around meal partner then, and it still is now.
**Wine Status: Still widely available, $14.99**

### Quinta do Ameal Loureiro Vinho Verde, Portugal
This bottle takes the Vinho Verde perspective from one dimension into three. And considering that the one dimension in itself is imminently enjoyable (see page 72), this is saying something. Just try it, and then I dare you to say that white wine is boring.
**Wine Status: Still widely available, $15.29**

### Chapoutier Bila Haut, France
The review on page 121 pretty much sums things up, but for nearly 15 years this has been a go-to bottle when gutsy red gets the call. File under: BBQ partner.
**Wine Status: Still widely available, $15.79**

### Tinhorn Creek Merlot, British Columbia
A benchmark for B.C. reds, it feels like Tinhorn's Merlot has been around forever (well, relatively forever in the context of the modern B.C. wine industry). Years back, this bottle proved to me that the province could produce rich, fulsome reds, and it still speaks nostalgically whenever it's poured into my glass.
**Wine Status: Still widely available, $17.39**

### Concha y Toro Marques de Casa Concha Chardonnay, Chile
Amidst all the talk of finesse and fine acidity, sometimes life calls for an unabashedly rich, borderline-trashy Chardonnay. That is when I reach for this bold bottle (which, despite its richness, comes across anything but cloying)—typically when a summer blockbuster is about to be screened and the popcorn is buttered.
**Wine Status: Still widely available, $17.49**

### Maison des Bulliats Regnie, France

I have a love/hate relationship with this wine. I hate it because it's a victim of its own deserved success. But I love it because it tastes so darn good. Quality Gamay, vis-à-vis Cru Beaujolais, continues to charm enthusiasts, which is good for the grape but bad for my pocketbook. Over the last decade I've seen Beaujolais prices steadily escalate, yet pound for pound, this wine still packs more real intensity and vibrancy than most any other bottle.

**Wine Status: Still widely available, $19.29**

### Wynns Coonawarra Riesling, Australia

I miss this Riesling. Riesling is one of my favourite grapes, and it's a touch tough to find super-delicious Riesling at a reasonable price. Which is what this bottle is—or, as it was described in the 2006 edition: "Wynns Riesling is a wine with a mission, laser-like in its focus on utter refreshment." Bone dry, lip-smacking, and crazy refreshing, it was a steal at 15 bucks when it was widely available, though it's still out there if you look a bit more thoroughly.

**Wine Status: Limited availability at private wine stores, $19.99**

### Donnafugata Anthìlia, Italy

To quote from the 2009 edition of Had a Glass: "It's hard to taste this wine. It's the sort of wine that's just so sumptuous, right from the first kiss on the lips that's so good you don't want to bother taking tasting notes or dealing with any other formalities."

**Wine Status: Limited availability at private wine stores, $26.49**

# Index by Country

The Royal Old Vines Chenin
   Blanc 58

## Spain
Alvear Medium Dry 160
Castillo de Almansa Riserva 107
El Petit Bonhomme Blanco 61
Jaume Serra Cristalino Brut
   Cava 144
Laya Old Vines Almansa 113
Lustau Puerto Fino Sherry 158
Luzada Albariño 75
Muga Rioja Rosado 94
Olivares Jumilla Rosado 89

Parés Baltà Brut Cava 149
Segura Viudas Brut Rosado Cava
   146
Villa Conchi Brut Selección Cava
   147
Vivanco Rioja Crianza 139

## United States
Chateau Ste. Michelle Riesling
   65
Quady Essensia Orange Muscat
   156
Robert Mondavi Winery Fumé
   Blanc 85

# Index by Type

Über Riesling Kabinett 69
Wakefield Riesling 82

**Rosé Blends**
Bieler Père et Fils Coteaux d'Aix-
en-Provence Rosé 93
Joie Rosé 96
Muga Rioja Rosado 94
Olivares Jumilla Rosado 89
Quails' Gate Rosé 92

**Sangiovese**
Castiglioni Chianti 119

**Sauvignon Blanc**
Babich Sauvignon Blanc 80
Casas del Bosque Reserva
Sauvignon Blanc 70
Casillero del Diablo Reserva
Sauvignon Blanc 54
Domaine Roc de Châteauvieux
Touraine 76
Marisco Vineyards The Ned
Sauvignon Blanc 67
Robert Mondavi Winery Fumé
Blanc 85

**Sherry**
Alvear Medium Dry 160
Lustau Puerto Fino Sherry 158

**Sovereign Opal**
Calona Vineyards Sovereign
Opal 52

**Sparkling Blends**
Marquis de la Tour Brut 145
See Ya Later Ranch SYL Brut 150

**Syrah / Shiraz**
Angove Family Winemakers
Nine Vines Grenache Shiraz
Rosé 91
Cave Saint Desirat Syrah 105
Yalumba Organic Shiraz 122

**Tempranillo**
Vivanco Rioja Crianza 139

**Torrontés**
Amaru High Vineyard Torrontés
Rosé 90
Crios de Susana Balbo Torrontés
64

**Verdejo**
El Petit Bonhomme Blanco 61

**Verdicchio**
Umani Ronchi Casal di Serra
Verdicchio Classico Superiore
84

**Viognier**
Le Paradou Viognier 59
Moillard Hugues le Juste
Viognier 62

**Vranac**
Plantaže Vranac 106

**White Blends**
Casal Garcia Vinho Verde 51
Wild Goose Autumn Gold 78

**Xinomavro**
Boutari Naoussa 120

# Acknowledgements

Given that this is the 10th Anniversary edition of Had a Glass, this year we'll keep to the 10 theme by way of a "Top 10" acknowledgements list. In no particular order, mind you, as this book relies upon the most amazing cohort of talented, creative, and supportive people around—all operating in a sort of human-Jenga fashion. Remove one and the entire Had a Glass franchise falls to pieces! Anyways, without further ado thanks is most certainly due to:

10. My loving wife, Karen, and high-energy daughters, Anika and Kaia, my favourite people with whom to enjoy good food, good conversation, and good wine (or apple juice, as the case may be).
9. Friends, new and old, and near or far, that are always willing to share a glass.
8. Kenji, my original partner in wine crime and the co-creator of Had a Glass. Though he now tills the soil and minds the grapes in France, this book remains as much a legacy of his creative energies.
7. Robert, Lindsay, Trish, and the entire Appetite and Penguin Random House Canada teams.
6. All the venues and editors that have long given me space to spread the wine love, notably The Province newspaper and TASTE magazine.
5. The grape growers, winemakers, wineries, agents, and wine shops going out of their way to ensure new and interesting wines find their way to my glass.
4. The colour grey.
3. Le Marché St. George, the best little neighbourhood grocer, which is my oasis in East Van (not to mention my selfless part-time porter), and not coincidentally is home to a couple of the most creative photographers/artists I know.
2. The grape Grolleau.
1. All you readers. Thanks to your curiosity and thirst, I am inspired to keep on swirling, sipping, and writing!

Klee Larsen

# About the Author

JAMES NEVISON is an award-winning wine writer, educator, and the co-founder of HALFAGLASS wine consultancy in Vancouver. James has co-authored ten bestselling wine books, and he is widely known as "The Wine Guy" from his weekly column in The Province newspaper. James also contributes regularly to TASTE magazine, and his casual and accessible take on wine is often heard and seen on radio and television. James has judged wine competitions in Canada and internationally, and in 2009 he was honoured to be named one of Western Living magazine's "Top 40 Foodies Under 40." (Oh, and he's still under 40!)

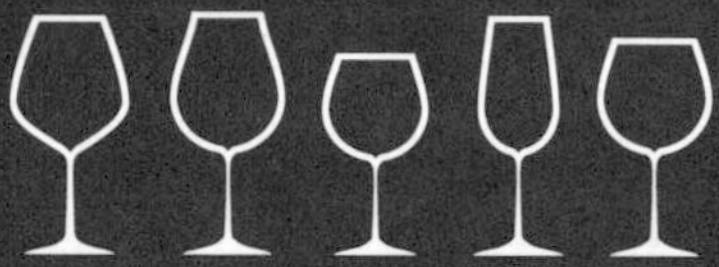